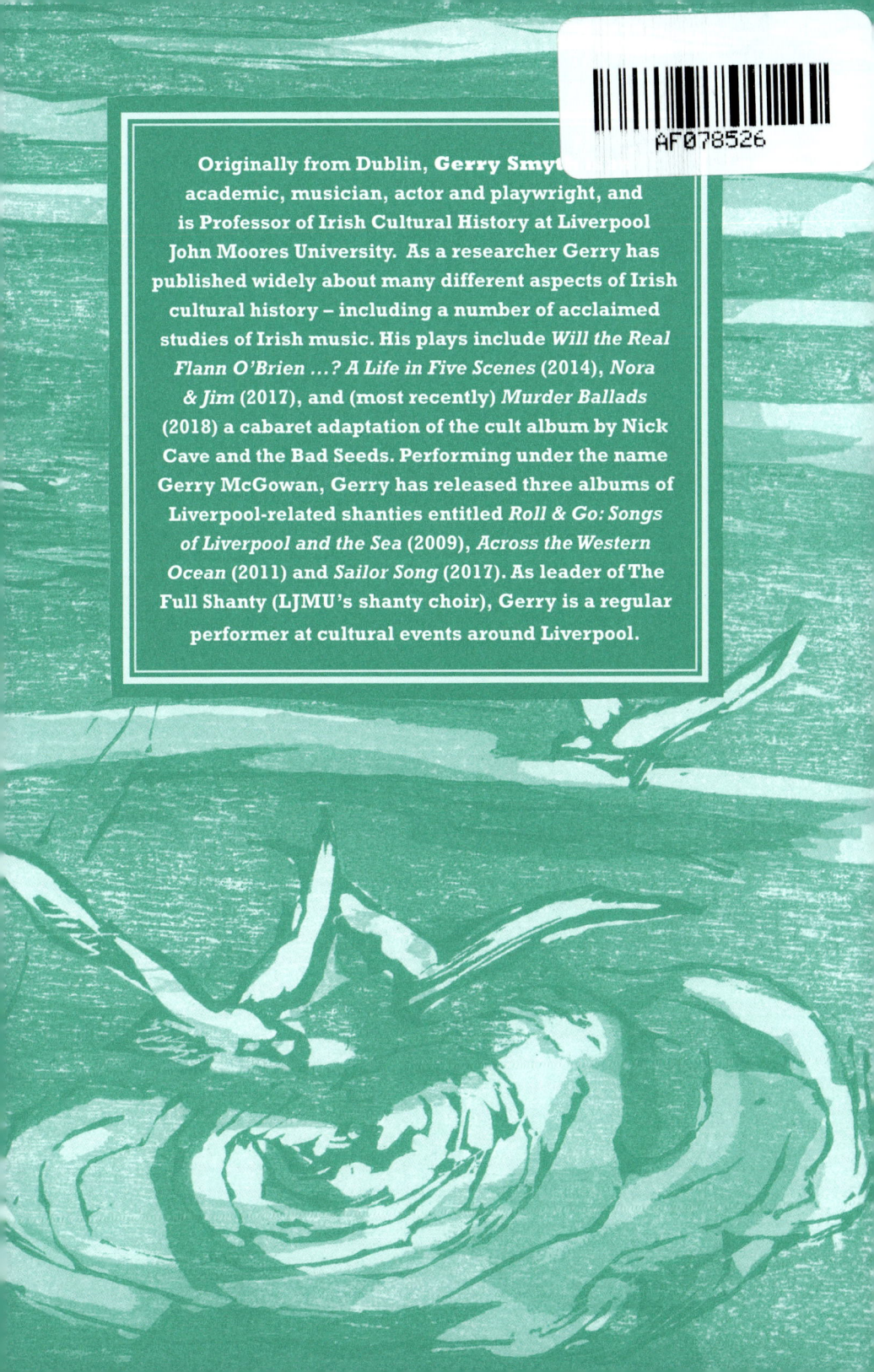

Originally from Dublin, **Gerry Smyth** is an academic, musician, actor and playwright, and is Professor of Irish Cultural History at Liverpool John Moores University. As a researcher Gerry has published widely about many different aspects of Irish cultural history – including a number of acclaimed studies of Irish music. His plays include *Will the Real Flann O'Brien …? A Life in Five Scenes* (2014), *Nora & Jim* (2017), and (most recently) *Murder Ballads* (2018) a cabaret adaptation of the cult album by Nick Cave and the Bad Seeds. Performing under the name Gerry McGowan, Gerry has released three albums of Liverpool-related shanties entitled *Roll & Go: Songs of Liverpool and the Sea* (2009), *Across the Western Ocean* (2011) and *Sailor Song* (2017). As leader of The Full Shanty (LJMU's shanty choir), Gerry is a regular performer at cultural events around Liverpool.

**Publisher's Note**

The shanties and ballads presented in this volume are historical texts, sung almost exclusively by working men on long, arduous, sea voyages, principally in the nineteenth and early twentieth centuries. These songs are of a genre which on occasion exhibits outdated, stereotyped, misogynistic and offensive language and sentiments. Whilst it would be impossible and misleading to present a history of sailor song without some reference to this language, the examples in this volume have been limited and each fully contextualised. The archaic and unacceptable views expressed in a small number of the song lyrics do not represent the opinions of the British Library or those of the author.

This edition first published in Great Britain 2021 by

The British Library
96 Euston Road
London NW1 2DB

First published in North America in 2020

ISBN 978 0 7123 5370 0

Text copyright © Gerry Smyth 2020
Volume copyright © The British Library Board 2020
Images copyright © The British Library Board and other named copyright holders 2020
Feature illustrations (as detailed on page 159) copyright © Jonny Hannah 2020

The author asserts the moral right to be identified as the author of this work

All rights reserved. No part of this book may be reproduced or transmitted in any form or by any means, electronic or mechanical including photocopying, recording or by any information storage and retrieval system without the prior permission of the publishers in writing

Every reasonable effort has been made to trace copyright holders of material reproduced in this book, but if any have been inadvertently overlooked the publishers would be glad to hear from them

British Library Cataloguing in Publication Data

A catalogue record for this publication is available from the British Library

Edited by Christopher Westhorp
Picture Research by Sally Nicholls
Designed by Nicola Bailey

Printed in Italy by Printer Trento Srl

# SAILOR SONG
## The Shanties and Ballads of the High Seas

### Gerry Smyth
### Illustrated by Jonny Hannah

# CONTENTS

| | |
|---|---|
| 6 | Introduction |
| 20 | A note on the material |

## THE SHANTIES

| | |
|---|---|
| 22 | 1. Across the Western Ocean |
| 24 | 2. A-Roving |
| 26 | 3. The Banks of the Sacramento |
| 28 | 4. The Black Ball Line |
| 30 | 5. Blood-Red Roses |

## Collectors and Editors

| | |
|---|---|
| 34 | 6. Blow the Man Down |
| 38 | 7. Boney Was a Warrior |
| 40 | 8. Bully in the Alley |
| 42 | 9. Can't You Dance the Polka? |
| 44 | 10. Cheer'ly Man |
| 46 | 11. Clear the Track, Let the Bullgine Run |

## Music and the Sea

| | |
|---|---|
| 50 | 12. The Dead Horse |
| 52 | 13. Drunken Sailor |
| 54 | 14. Fire Down Below |
| 56 | 15. Goodbye, Fare-Ye-Well |
| 58 | 16. Hanging Johnny |
| 60 | 17. Haul Away, Joe |

## Themes and Dreams

| | |
|---|---|
| 66 | 18. Haul on the Bowline |
| 68 | 19. The Hog-Eye Man |
| 70 | 20. John Kanaka |
| 72 | 21. Johnny Boker |
| 74 | 22. Leave Her, Johnny, Leave Her |

## Sailortown

| | |
|---|---|
| 78 | 23. Liverpool Judies |
| 80 | 24. Lowlands Away |
| 82 | 25. Paddy Doyle's Boots |
| 84 | 26. Paddy, Lay Back |
| 86 | 27. Reuben Ranzo |
| 88 | 28. Rio Grande |

| | | |
|---|---|---|
| 90 | **Bawdy** | |
| 92 | 29. | Roll, *Alabama*, Roll |
| 94 | 30. | Sally Brown |
| 96 | 31. | Santiana |
| 98 | 32. | Shallow Brown |
| 100 | 33. | Shenandoah |
| 102 | 34. | So Handy, My Girls |
| 104 | 35. | South Australia |
| 106 | **Folk or Fake?** | |
| 108 | 36. | Stormalong John |
| 110 | 37. | Tom's Gone to Hilo |
| 112 | 38. | We're All Bound to Go |
| 114 | 39. | Whip Jamboree |
| 116 | 40. | Whisky Johnny |
| 118 | **Stan Hugill** | |

## THE BALLADS AND SONGS

| | | |
|---|---|---|
| 122 | 1. | The Banks of Newfoundland |
| 126 | 2. | Canadee-i-o |
| 130 | 3. | Do Me Ama |
| 132 | 4. | The *Dreadnought* |
| 134 | 5. | The *Flying Cloud* |
| 136 | **(Rock 'n') Roll and Go** | |
| 138 | 6. | Go to Sea Once More |
| 140 | 7. | High Barbaree |
| 142 | 8. | The Leaving of Liverpool |
| 146 | 9. | Maggie May |
| 150 | 10. | Spanish Ladies |
| 152 | **The Shanty Today** | |

| | |
|---|---|
| 154 | Glossary |
| 156 | Further Reading and Listening |
| 157 | Notes |
| 159 | Picture Credits and Illustration Information |
| 160 | Acknowledgements |

# Introduction

Ship heaved and sea heaved, and there were sounds
    in the heaves.
Sing a song, ship cried, sing a song, sailor, cried sea.
Sing as I go down, sing as I heave up.
**James Hanley,** *Sailor's Song*

This singing art is sea foam.
The graceful movements come from a pearl
somewhere on the ocean floor.
**Rumi, 13th-century Persian Poet**

The shanty is a form of work song that developed on the commercial vessels which sailed the world's seas during the nineteenth century. There is some dispute as to the term's origin and (as a consequence) its spelling. The earliest dictionary entry is from 1869; and while some authorities suggest that it derives from the portable 'shanty' houses common throughout the Caribbean islands, another possibility is that it's an adaptation of the French word *chanter*, meaning 'to sing'. In fact, 'chanter' as a synonym for 'singer' has been in continual use throughout Britain since the Middle Ages. Whatever the case, many people favoured 'chantey' over 'shanty' until the latter eventually won through in the middle decades of the twentieth century.

Why do people sing when they work? The ancient and universal practice seems to have two major benefits. Firstly, music's rhythmic properties enable people engaged in group activities to co-ordinate their efforts, and thus to deploy the available energy in a more efficient manner. Secondly, by providing access to a range of properties and effects not readily available in everyday life (harmony, melody, rhyme, rhythm, and so on), singing boosts physical resilience and psychological well-being. Any task requiring arduous and/or repetitive group activity can probably be performed more efficiently to musical

Sovereign of the Sea,
*engraving by Jacques
La Grange, 1936.*

accompaniment. Without straying too far into the realm of psychology, I would go further and say that such is especially the case if that accompaniment is organised or 'controlled' to some degree by the workers themselves, thereby affording some form of agency beyond the merely functional task in which they are employed.

## Global commerce

A quarter-century of international conflict on land and at sea ended with the Battle of Waterloo (1815), after which the way opened for the expansion of global trade and travel. The shanty historian and singer Stan Hugill (see page 118) identified 1818 as the moment of 'take-off', for it was in that year that an American shipping company named the Black Ball Line commenced a regular run between New York and Liverpool, sailing on the first of each month, irrespective of the weather or amount of cargo loaded. The journey took 23 days for the

*North Quay, Drogheda, Ireland, c.1860–1883.*

The *Great Western* of the US Black Ball Line, by Antonio Jacobsen, 1916.

eastward trip, about 40 coming back; and although probably few realised it at the time, this schedule contributed importantly to a new phase in the development of modern capitalism.

Other 'lines' followed in quick succession: Swallowtail, Red Star, Dramatic, Black Cross. Some failed, some succeeded, but the viability of the route had been established. Increased trade and the need for greater speed necessitated the design of a new type of vessel: the high-speed, three-masted, square-rigged clipper. Tonnage and sail yardage continued to increase throughout the middle decades of the century. The foundation of Lloyd's Register of Shipping in 1834 and the repeal of the Navigation Acts in 1849 contributed to a context in which trade could flourish, with still more ships leading to more passages and greater commerce.

One thing that did not necessarily increase, however, was crew size. Fewer men working harder and longer made commercial sense; a 2,000-tonne ship, for example, might be expected to operate with a crew of no more than 30 hands. This was the context within which the modern sea shanty evolved and thrived. The Marxist folk singer and historian A.L. (Bert) Lloyd was in no doubt that '[the] modern form of capitalism that gave rise to the great shipping lines produced at the same time the striking body of primitive folk songs that we call: sea shanties'.

It seems, incidentally, that Anglophone shanty-singing was restricted by and large to merchant vessels. The Royal Navy and United States Navy operated according to a different system in which efficiency and discipline were based on the strict observation of a specialised system of signals, codes and protocols.

## The shantyman

Work on board the typical merchant ship consisted in large part of a variety of heavy physical tasks – raising the anchor, hoisting and adjusting sails, pumping bilge water, and so forth. It was soon observed that sailors operated more efficiently when working to a rhythm that was sympathetic to the task in hand. This was the context within which the practical benefits of the co-ordinated work song became apparent.

One recurring format was the call-and-response song, which works like this: an experienced individual chooses an appropriate song to accompany the job in hand, and after some preliminary shouts or cries (a sing-out) to announce what that song is, he sings the first line alone (solo). The second (response) line is then sung by the work gang, during which a joint physical effort (a pull or a heave) takes place, timed to coincide with a particular emphasis (lyrical and/or musical) in the song itself. This pattern continues until the job is completed, and the soloist announces that the workers may cease their efforts.

Another name for the soloist who organised this activity was 'shantyman'. He was generally an experienced hand who thoroughly understood shipboard work, and who had the respect of officers and crew. 'Shantyman' was an informal designation but an important one for both the efficient management of the ship and the well-being of the manual workers. Richard Runciman Terry writes: 'The importance of the shantyman could not be overestimated. A good shantyman with a pretty wit was worth his weight in gold. He was a privileged person, and was excused all work save light or odd jobs.' A strong voice and an ability to improvise content could earn a sailor a bonus on top of his normal pay.

## The tempo of teamwork

But how did the sailors know precisely when to undertake the required physical action – the heaving or the hauling? Here's an example adapted from one given to the collector Cecil Sharp by an experienced sailor at the beginning of the twentieth century:

*I sell brooms, squeegees and swabs*

Imagine that line being chanted by a dozen or more people, to a strong underlying rhythm (**1**-and-**2**-and-**3**-and-**4**-and-**1**-and-**2**-and-**3**-and-**4**-and), with minor preparatory pulses on **broo** and **squee**, before everyone undertakes the exact same physical action (a single pull on a rope, for example on **SWABS**). Now we have something like this:

The disposition of syllables and stresses in relation to the rest of the rhythm doesn't really matter – only the point at which the joint physical action takes place. So, in relation to one of the well-known shanties included in this volume, this particular pattern could be rendered something like this:

If the line is repeated over and over, we find that the emphases start to drift, so although the underlying rhythm remains the same, the stresses now come in different places:

Now we have *two* main stresses (**BROO** and **SWAB**), which means that we can have *two* focused action points within the same line:

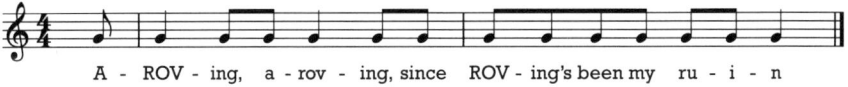

This same pattern, moreover, can be adapted to different rhythms – three (or six) beats to the bar, for example:

Transposed into familiar shanty format, we have something like this:

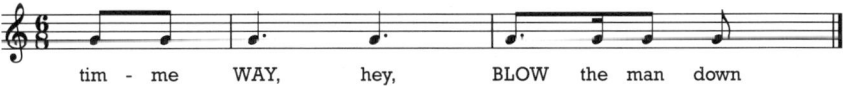

The point is that everyone involved in the activity knows precisely when and where the physical effort must be made, and they may prepare themselves accordingly. The kinetic energy thus generated is greater than would be otherwise available; there's time to recover between pulls, and the job is suddenly much easier than it would be if it were just a bunch of guys pulling a rope at different times, to separate rhythms. Concentration is increased, boredom is allayed, morale is improved – importantly, resentment at the fact that there are probably too few men for the task in hand is abated. In short, the shanties provided a rhythm to improve efficiency through 'concerted' effort – a word that, with its connotations of collaboration and performance, seems particularly apt.

### Capstan and halyard songs

So, a series of song forms emerged, each designed to support one or other of the shipboard chores necessary for the efficient running of these bigger, faster vessels. Although 'tight categories are misleading', as Lloyd points out, 'in the earlier, formative years of the modern shanty, the nature of the job in hand and the gestures needed to fulfil it were important, even decisive, in shaping the melody, rhythm, metre and tempo of the songs'. Stan Hugill describes two main types and their subdivisions:

*Sailors working on deck, ship and date unknown.*

*The capstan song and the halyard song. The capstan song was subdivided into: a) the windlass, or anchor capstan shanty, b) the capstan song, sung when doing a job-o-work other than heaving the anchor ... The halyard shanty, used for hoisting sails, was subdivided into: a) long pulls; b) foresheeters; c) buntstowers ... For pumping it was considered any old sea-song would do, so long as it had a good grand chorus.*

The two main types identified here by Hugill refer to two of the principal physical actions of which the human body is capable – pushing and

*Sailors securing a section of the foresail, which had come free in heavy weather, on board the ship Garthsnaid, 1920.*

pulling, or, in maritime parlance, *heaving* and *hauling*. Capstan songs are associated with heaving – for example, by pushing at the bars which turned a mushroom-shaped winch in order to raise the anchor. This was an arduous task, which could occupy an entire ship's company over an extended period – sometimes a whole day or more. The capstan was superseded around the middle of the nineteenth century by the more efficient 'brake-windlass', whose different mechanism required a different kind of effort, resulting in the evolution of a different kind of shanty. The monotonous task of pumping bilge water from these leaky wooden vessels was the most unpopular shipboard task, and it too developed its own particular canon of work songs.

Halyard songs were associated with pulling (*hauling*) ropes in order to raise heavy sails. Whereas heaving songs were mainly used for jobs requiring an action that was continuous and regular, hauling songs were sung during tasks which required breaks. There are variations on each of these basic actions, of course, depending on the technology available and the precise nature of the task at hand. One could, for example, pull in one continuous motion, pull intermittently, pull hand-over-hand, or turn around and 'walk away' from the pulled object. To this day there is no strict, final taxonomy for all the different kinds of shipboard work song.

## Downtime

Singing was one of the principal forms of free entertainment available in a predominantly oral culture. Besides the extensive canon of work songs, nineteenth-century merchant seamen were also evidently fond of singing when off duty. These songs were sung at the 'bits' – large wooden cleats to which ropes were attached, towards the front of the ship; hence they were commonly known as 'forebitters' (or 'mainhatch' songs on American vessels). The predominant form was the ballad – a narrative in which the structure and melody of each verse is repeated throughout. Many genres were popular, however: composed love songs of the period, traditional drinking songs, music hall hits, and so on. Many accounts exist of singing sessions with each off-duty sailor being called on to make a contribution; and a good deal of time and thought has been devoted to understanding the relationship between the forebitter and the shanty proper.

Not all of these forebitters were *about* the sea or maritime matters, of course; but it's interesting to observe that the 'nautical ballad' proliferates in the British folk song tradition, and that there are hundreds of songs about different aspects of sea life: pirating, slaving, fishing, pressganging, emigrating, whaling, and so forth. There is an extensive sub-category all on its own for the 'lover gone to (or lost at) sea'. In The Ballads and Songs (see pages 120–151) the importance of this aspect of nineteenth-century maritime culture is acknowledged.

As far as the shanty work song is concerned, according to Lloyd the practice of shanty-singing as we know it emerged during the American-dominated packet ships of, roughly, 1830–50, and it 'reached its peak in the British-dominated clipper-ship era of 1855–70'. As a living tradition it was in serious decline by about 1880 in the face of competition from steam-driven ships.

*Below and opposite: Examples of 'Jolly Sailor' Victorian Valentine cards. 1845–50.*

Frank, generous, brave, a Sailor's soul,
Links all his friends from pole to pole;
Come then, in Wedlock's bands let's join,
I'll love till death my Valentine.

## In search of the authentic

As soon as its demise was imminent, shanty-singing began to attract the attention of folklorists. These men and women were determined to identify and preserve as much of the original material as possible. Such determination, however, raised the spectre of *authenticity* which has haunted shanty research ever since – the conviction that these songs could not meaningfully exist outside the context within which they had first developed, and that even the most sympathetic attempt to reproduce the shanty outwith its natural environment was in some sense complicit with the modernising forces which had combined to render the form obsolete, leading to ignorant landlubbers being upbraided for their 'perversions' of the original practice.

The El Dorado of 'authenticity' is a notoriously difficult concept to locate – much valued, always desired, always elusive (see Folk or Fake, pages 106–107). In the present context, authenticity is compromised by the radical discrepancy between the original singing context and the various performance and stylistic contexts within which the shanty subsequently fetched up. Even Stan Hugill, the most tolerant of commentators, once complained that 'shore singers of shanties rarely manage to get the right "atmosphere" into their offerings; they are not raucous or strident enough'. Attempting to define the original style with reference to particular qualities or techniques is ultimately unviable: it was the context of gang work that generated the specific 'atmosphere' in which the shanty was sung, and that context was less and less available after the advent of steam.

## Origins and essence

Where did the shanties come from? The answer is: anywhere and everywhere. As Lloyd suggests, the shanties were composed under the influence of many places:

*The melodies are a fine jumble of pentatonic phrases that may have derived originally from Gaelic or African culture, modal formulas from the English countryside, and modern commonplaces from stage hits of the first half of Victoria's reign.*

The poetic improvisations of the shantymen, likewise, were inspired by images and phrases adapted from a wide range of European and African languages, 'along with tags invented by the yelping comedians of the time on both sides of the Atlantic'.

Hugill concurs, describing an eclectic range of sources and influences, including long-established hauling cries, dance tunes, folk songs and ballads (American and European as well as British); adapted art music, including custom-composed martial

Watching the Height of the Waves, *published in* The Graphic, *18 March, 1871.*

music of varying kinds; hymns, and popular songs. There seems no doubt, however, that the two most important influences on the development of the shanty were African-American sources (including call-and-response work songs associated with the Gulf of Mexico ports of the American Deep South and the Atlantic ports of Virginia, the Carolinas and Florida, as well as West Indian and Latin American contributions) and, most consistently from Hugill's perspective, Ireland.

Someday, someone will write a book about the shanty's enduring attraction for people far removed in time and space from the contexts in which these simple work songs emerged. When they do, they will have to consider issues such as the significance of the Atlantic as the cradle (perhaps 'womb' is a better image) of modernity in political, economic and ideological terms. They will also have to consider issues such as the mutual advance of capitalism and the nation-state, as well as the transition from a predominantly oral to a predominantly literate culture. In more general terms, that writer will have to acknowledge the central significance of the sea for the human imagination – the seven-tenths of its global presence echoed in the seven-tenths of each individual's bodily composition. The ocean haunts us, as James Hamilton-Paterson writes, because 'the salt which is in seawater is in our blood, sweat and tears'.

Most importantly, that writer will have to consider the power of the shanty to articulate something essential about the human condition – the way in which, for all their crudeness of form and banality of content, these songs manage to speak to (well, sing to) something primordial about what it means to be alive with a body that *feels*, a mind that *thinks* and a spirit that *yearns*.

Something of that miraculous, elemental condition is captured by Charlotte Runcie's description, in her book *Salt on Your Tongue* (2019), of shanty-singing in a seaside pub near Edinburgh:

*The lights dim. Someone has lit some candles and placed them onto the pub's mantelpiece. Through the window, the waves are moving gently on the horizon, over the heads of the choir as they start to sing. Away, lads, away, away for Rio! ... It's our version of a sea shanty, a shorebound telling of the hardships of sea, the only version we are capable of making.*

*Evening falls calm and mild as the light of the water fades to indigo. If you were standing outside the pub that night, all you would hear would be songs and the splash of waves.*

I hope the readers of this book may hear the splash of waves in the songs, and the silence beyond.

*Illustration from the front cover of 'The Keel Row Schottische', composed by J.G. Jones, 1873.*

# A note on the material

As pointed out in the Introduction, the idea of an 'authentic', 'proper' or 'real' shanty remains problematic. This in turn presents a number of issues for my principal purpose here, which is to provide singable versions of some of the shanties and sea songs that have survived into the present. In the end, this comes down to a series of editorial choices relating to repertoire, lyrics and melody – all based to a greater or lesser degree on the work of previous contributors to the field.

The 40 shanties included here are intended to be indicative of the range of material that was extant in the Anglophone maritime tradition at some point during the nineteenth century. Because the same shanty could be adapted for different tasks and contexts, the material is in alphabetical order rather than in terms of their different shipboard functions – for example, capstan shanties, halyard shanties, and so forth.

Collectors of a more musical bent have been much exercised by the presence within shanty music (and folk music generally) of the 'modes' – a vernacular music system predating the 12-tone equal temperament of classical tonality. In practice, most shanties fit fairly straightforwardly into the minor/major key division with which all modern folk and art musicians will be familiar.

The idea of using musical notation to transcribe any genre of folk or popular music is problematic in all sorts of ways. Earlier collectors provided musical transcriptions because there were fewer opportunities to hear the material itself. Most people now have access (via the Internet) to more or less the entire shanty canon in multiple versions; for that reason, the transcriptions provided here represent the bare bones of one ideal version of any given song.

The musical notation is rendered as simply as possible in each case. All the provided melodies are pitched in the key of C major (no sharps or flats), with any deviating notes indicated as accidentals in the text. I'm happy to leave it to singers to transpose these melodies into sympathetic keys. Neither have I made any attempt to notate the various stylistic traits which, for some people, characterise 'authentic' shanty-singing – whoops and yelps, or the extraordinary 'hitches' which announced the shanty's commencement. I've made no indication of the way in which solo and refrain might overlap.

All time signatures have been as standardised as possible – a process which has called for some invention, and in one or two instances ('Lowlands Away', for example, or 'Shallow Brown') a leap of musical faith. My attempt to retain the 'lilt' of the original material seems to have produced an inordinate number of triplets – three equally weighted counts over two beats – compared with the musical transcribers of yesteryear.

With regard to all these musical attributes, I would simply note once again that, because it's invariably an aesthetic *judgment* rather than an objective *quality*, the category of 'authenticity' comes with the inevitable scare quotes.

Stan Hugill maintained that harmony was rare to non-existent for the working sailor, and one can understand why: a man would have had things other than 'thirds' and 'fifths' to think of when raising a heavy sail in strong wind and rain. But experienced singers will find extensive harmonic possibilities throughout these songs, just as some of the popular modern shanty groups (such as Fisherman's Friends or Kimber's Men) have introduced effective harmony into their renditions.

Lyrics are the most awkward category of all – and not just for the fact (as pointed out in the section on 'Bawdy') that the preserved words are in many instances probably very different to the ones that would have been sung at sea. The aesthetic properties of the shanty – incorporating extemporisation, interchangeable 'tags' (stock lines and phrases), macaronic and nonsense terms, and so forth – simply do not answer the requirements of the authoritative text. This volume is intended to be *indicative* rather than *comprehensive*; when it comes to the shanty (and, to a lesser extent, the sea ballad) there are simply too many verses, too much interchangeability, too much guesswork, too much invention.

For present purposes I have followed my own singing/arranging practice (developed over a number of years) in compiling a composite lyric which I believe makes each song a successful event in and of itself. Punctuation has been kept to a minimum, and except for cases in which pronunciation outranks sense, spelling has been standardised. Solo lines are rendered in roman type, collective responses and choruses in indented italics; after the first verse, only the solo lines are given.

I hope you enjoy singing these beautiful songs that have come down to us from the great days of sail.

PORTSMOUT
RUEBEN RANZO
PARADISE STREET
KANAKA
ALABAMA
1822
ALPHABET DE LA MARINE
THE SHANTIES
HUGILL
SHENANDOAH
PACKET RAT
JOANNA COLCORD
CAPE HORN
Mustard Plaster CURES ALL
SAILOR TOWN
DRUNKEN SAILOR
BLACK BALL
MARX
A.L. lloyd
the HORN BOOK
G.LEGMAN
SOUTH AUSTRALIA

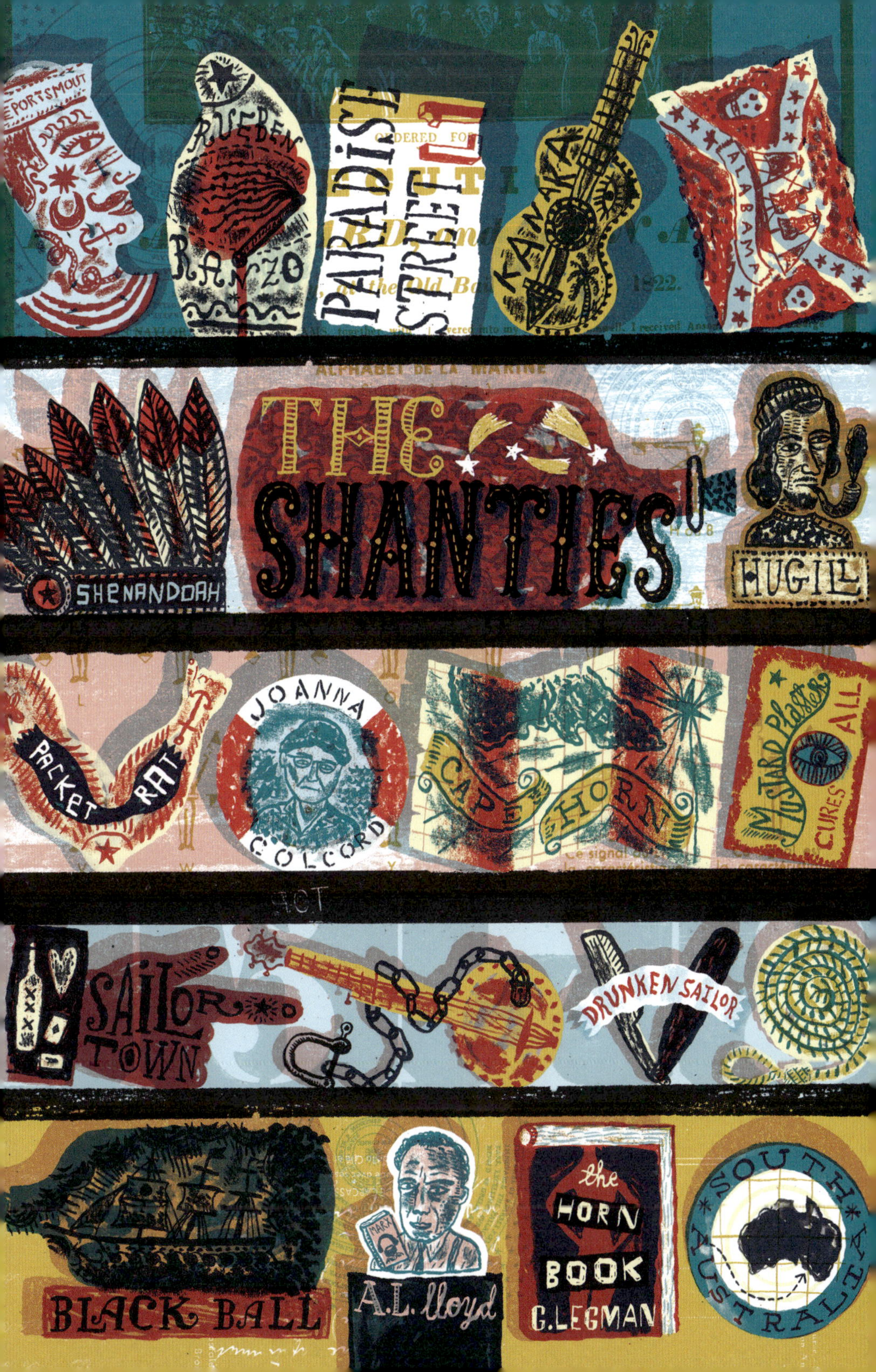

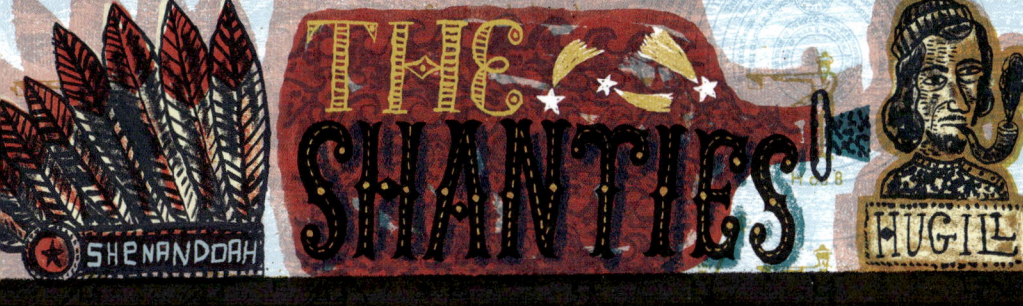

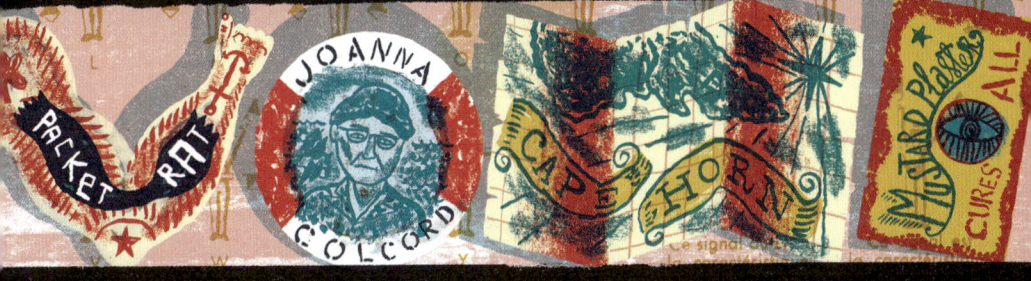

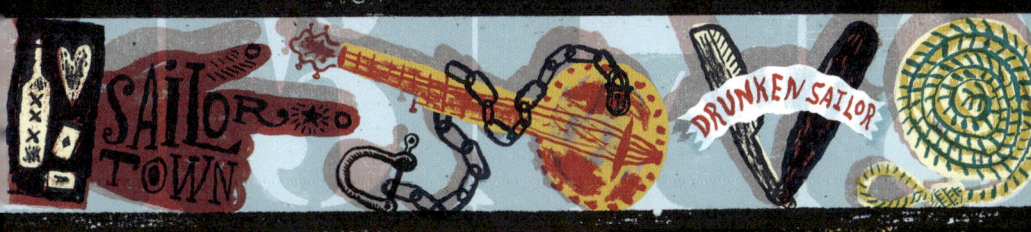

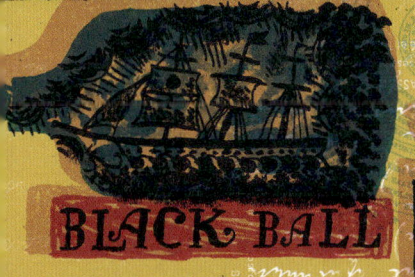

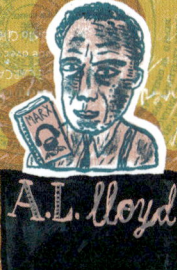

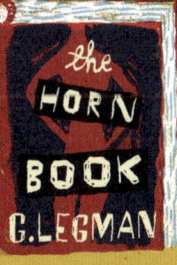

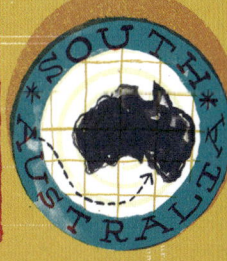

# 1. ACROSS THE WESTERN OCEAN

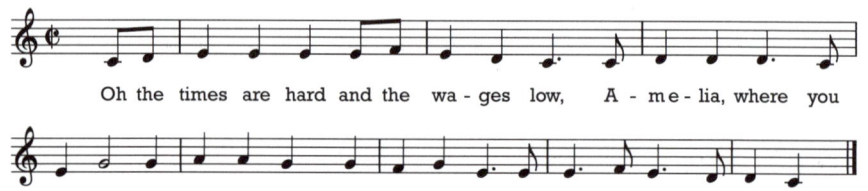

Oh the times are hard and the wa-ges low, A-me-lia, where you bound to? The Roc-ky Moun-tains are my home, A-cross the West-ern O-cean

Oh the times are hand and the wages low
  *Amelia, where you bound to?*
The Rocky Mountains are my home
  *Across the Western Ocean*

A land of promise there you'll see
  *Amelia, where you bound to?*
I'm bound across that western sea
  *To join the Irish army*

To Liverpool I'll make my way
Liverpool, that Yankee school

There's Liverpool Pat with his tarpaulin hat
And Yankee Jack, that Packet Rat

Beware those packet ships, I say
They'll steal your goods and clothes away

Mothers and sweethearts don't you cry
Sisters and brothers say goodbye

**C**aptain Whall dates this shanty to about 1850, and links it with the wave of Irish emigration to North America (many of whom travelled via Liverpool across the Atlantic, or Western, Ocean) resulting from the Great Famine of the late-1840s. Stan Hugill accepts Whall's suggestion that 'Amelia' is an adaptation of O'Melia, although the latter is not in fact such a common Irish name. In *Irish Ballads and Songs of the Sea*, James Healy claims that the 'Irish army' of the second verse was in fact 'the brigade, largely Fenian in sentiment, being raised by men such as [Thomas Francis] Meagher in America during the civil war there'. In any event, some of the pathos of the emigrant ballad survives in the final image of enforced farewell to loved ones.

According to Hugill, 'Packet Rat' refers to 'probably the toughest seamen salt water has ever known'. In time it became a generic designation for transatlantic sailors of Irish extraction hailing from the great emigrant destinations of Liverpool, New York and Boston. This association may help to account for the presence of so many traditional Irish melodies among the maritime music (forebitters and ballads as well as shanties) of the nineteenth century.

Whall identifies this song as a progenitor of the better-known hauling shanty 'Leave Her, Johnny, Leave Her' (No. 22). In slightly altered formats, 'Across the Western Ocean' was used for sail hauling, pumping and probably capstan heaving as well. Like many shanties, in fact, it was a versatile, multipurpose vehicle which could be adapted for different ends.

Poor Jack, *illustration by George Cruikshank, from Charles Dibden's* Songs Naval and National, *1841.*

# 2. A-ROVING

In Amsterdam there lived a maid
*Mark well what I do say*
In Amsterdam there lived a maid
And she was mistress of her trade
*I'll go no more a-roving with you, fair maid*
*A-roving, a-roving, since roving's been my ru-i-en*
*I'll go no more a-roving with you fair maid*

I met this fair maid after dark
And took her to her favourite park

I put my arm around her waist
Says she 'Young man, you're in great haste!'

I put my hand upon her thigh
Says she 'Young man, you're rather high!'

I took that girl upon my knee
Says she 'Young man, you're rather free!'

She swore that she'd be true to me
But spent me pay-day fast and free

In three weeks' time I was badly bent
So off to sea I sadly went

And then back to the Liverpool Docks
Saltpetre stowed in me boots and socks

Now when I got back home from sea
A soldier had her on his knee

Taking in Sail, *engraving by Jacques La Grange, 1936.*

**A**lso known as 'Roving', 'Amsterdam' or sometimes 'The Maid of Amsterdam', this old song (telling a *very* old story) has a highly dispersed genealogy, and an even more diverse set of intertextual influences.[1]

Part of the song's enduring attraction must lie in its universal theme and its endless adaptability: 'Amsterdam', for example, could be replaced by 'Liverpool', 'London Town', or wherever. Likewise, the encounter, the seduction and the comic pay-off can be spun out in many different ways, according to the performance context and the ingenuity of the singer.

Lloyd writes that 'A-Roving' was originally a land ballad adapted for capstan heaving. The burden of the long shanty version was 'frankly Rabelaisian', as Hugill put it; the reference to Amsterdam (then, as now, a centre for commercial vice) is an early clue. The maid's acquiescence to the sailor's exploration of more-and-more intimate parts of her anatomy – 'coarse and indelicate', according to Sampson – would certainly have shocked late-nineteenth-century collectors.

# 3. THE BANKS OF THE SACRAMENTO

As I was roll-ing down the Strand, Hoo-dah! Hoo-dah! I met two fair-ies hand-in-hand, Hoo-dah, Hoo-dah, day! Blow, boy-s, blow for Cal-i-for-ni-o, There's plen-ty of gold, so I've been told on the banks of the Sa-cram-en-to

As I was rolling down the Strand,
   *Hoodah! Hoodah!*
I met two fairies hand-in-hand
   *Hoodah, hoodah day!*

CHORUS:
*Blow, boys, blow for Californio
There's plenty of gold, so I've been told
On the banks of the Sacramento*

I chose the one with the curly locks
She let me chase her o'er the rocks

I chased her high, I chased her low
I fell down and broke my toe

Off to the doctor I did go
And I showed him my big toe

In came the nurse with a mustard poultice
Banged it on, but I took no notice

Now I'm well and free from pain
I'll never court flash girls again

*Sailing card for the clipper ship* California, *depicting scenes from the California Gold Rush, c.1850.*

**T**his is the first of a number of shanties incorporating a singalong chorus in addition to verses based on the usual call-and-response format. Sometimes these choruses evolved in the work environment, if the job-at-hand allowed; sometimes they were added later.

This was a popular capstan shanty, available in many versions, whose origins are much debated. The melody and the 'Hoodah' refrain suggest a reworking of 'Camptown Races' by Stephen Foster – the American songwriter (of Irish/Scottish descent) whose other notable compositions included 'Oh Susanna' and 'Hard Times', as well as sentimental favourites such as 'Jeanie With the Light Brown Hair' and 'Beautiful Dreamer'.

'Camptown Races' was a blackface minstrel song first published in 1850. The debate (about which all the major shanty researchers have had their say) relates to the song's potential African-American origins, as well as the question of whether the shanty pre-dated Foster's composition or vice versa.[2]

Blackface minstrelsy was a musical craze originating in the United States in the 1840s; its influence was extensive and pervasive. It was, as Steve Roud writes, 'the first of the American song fads to sweep Britain' – and while certainly not the last, it was possibly the least salubrious.

The shanty's chorus adverts to the Californian Gold Rush of the 1840s–50s, whereas the verses place it within the sub-genre of songs dealing (comically or tragically) with sexually transmitted disease. This is a theme which we shall encounter again.

I have chosen the place-name title here because there exists another, very different shanty (not included in this volume) bearing this entry's alterative name of 'Blow, Boys, Blow'.

# 4. THE BLACK BALL LINE

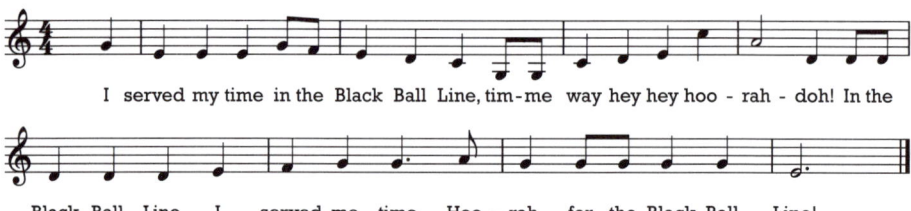

I served my time in the Black Ball Line, tim-me way hey hey hoo-rah-doh! In the Black Ball Line I served me time, Hoo-rah for the Black Ball Line!

I served my time in the Black Ball Line
*Timme way hey hey hoorah-doh!*
In the Black Ball Line I served me time
*Hoorah for the Black Ball Line!*

The Black Ball ships are good and true
They are the ships for me and you

Once there was a Black Ball ship
Fourteen knots an hour could clip

You will surely find a rich gold mine
Just take a trip in the Black Ball Line

Just take a trip to Liverpool
To Liverpool, that Yankee school

The Yankee sailors you'll see there
With red top boots and short cut hair

There's Liverpool Pat with his tarpaulin hat
And Paddy McGee the Packet Rat

As mentioned in the Introduction, the American Black Ball Line was one of the first commercial ventures to ply the Atlantic trade between Liverpool and New York in the years after the Napoleonic Wars. Stan Hugill refers throughout his *Shanties from the Seven Seas* to 'the Blackball line'; and the matter is confused even further by the existence of an Australian Blackball Line as well as the launching of a separate 'Black Ball Line' out of Liverpool in 1851. In any event, the original Yankee venture was, according to Bert Lloyd, a chastening school for merchant sailors, with discipline tight to the point of brutality. To be able to claim work experience aboard a Black Ball ship was an indication of courage, perhaps stupidity, but pride also, and certainly an ability to survive in adverse conditions. The notorious Black Ball became part of nineteenth-century sailing culture, with references popping up in many other shanties.

Although there are claims for its being used at halyards, Lloyd describes 'The Black Ball Line' as 'one of the most rousing of heaving shanties, with a rhythm particularly apt for work at the old-fashioned spokewindlass such as Black Ball ships used before 1840'. The version included here was sung by the great Ewan MacColl on a recording entitled *Farewell Nancy*, released by the folk label Topic in 1964. It includes some of the stock formulations – 'Liverpool Pat with his tarpaulin hat', for example – that fetch up in a host of other shanties (including its close relative 'Blow the Man Down', No. 6), and establishes the port of Liverpool as one of the key co-ordinates of the international maritime imagination.

# 5. BLOOD-RED ROSES

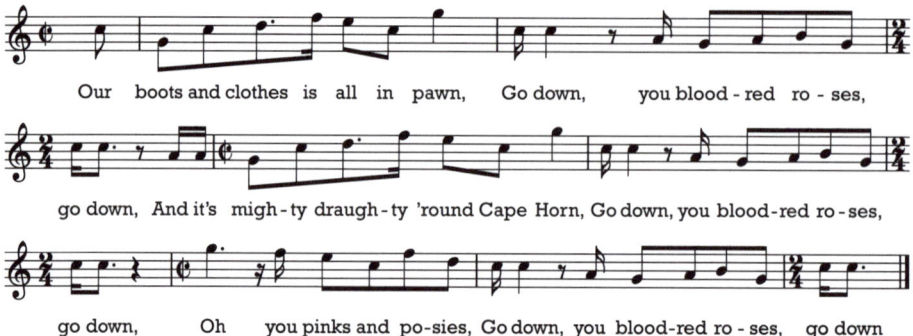

Our boots and clothes is all in pawn, Go down, you blood-red ro-ses, go down, And it's migh-ty draugh-ty 'round Cape Horn, Go down, you blood-red ro-ses, go down, Oh you pinks and po-sies, Go down, you blood-red ro-ses, go down

Our boots and clothes is all in pawn
*Go down, you blood-red roses, go down*
And it's mighty draughty 'round Cape Horn
*Go down, you blood-red roses, go down*
Oh you pinks and posies
*Go down, you blood-red roses, go down*

It's round that Cape we all must go
For that is where the whalefish blow
Oh you pinks and posies

Around Cape Stiff we all must go
Around Cape Stiff through the ice and snow
Oh you pinks and posies

Oh my old mother she wrote to me
My dearest son, come home from sea
Oh you pinks and posies

It's growl you may but go you must
If you growl too hard your head they'll bust
Oh you pinks and posies

Just one more pull and that'll do
For we're the boys to kick her through
Oh you pinks and posies

A Hundred Tons of Despair are Churning the Oceans, *illustration by A. Webb in The Idler, 1892.*

**T**his long-drag halyard shanty is unusual in terms of its structure – three solo lines and three refrains, the latter quite oddly phrased. Stan Hugill knew this song as 'Bunch o' Roses' with a four-part solo-refrain structure and a lyric based on the unlovable trade of South American nitrate and guano transportation (besides the smell, the raw material – seabird excrement – was difficult to collect and dangerous to transport). He also believed that although the 'roses' motif is borrowed from the English folk song tradition, the 'blood-red' reference in this instance may refer to the traditional red coats of the British Army. The 'roses' and 'posies' conjunction suggests a connection with the rhyme 'Ring a Ring o' Roses', which was popular in Britain and the United States in the later nineteenth century.

The lyric included here is a composite of different versions performed by Bert Lloyd, including the one he sang in the John Huston film *Moby Dick* (1956), starring Gregory Peck and Orson Welles. The pop singer Sting (formerly of the Police) performs a version of 'Blood Red Roses' on another album with a filmic connection, *Rogue's Gallery* (2006).[3]

The group with which I sing refuses to attempt 'Blood-Red Roses' in the 4/4 time signature I give here. The song, they maintain, requires the freedom bestowed by live performance, with the different voices working off each other in a super-sensitive exchange of call and response. The same could be said of all the shanties included in this volume.

# Collectors and Editors

In his magnificent *Folk Song in England* (2017) Steve Roud explores the contributions of the early collectors and editors of folk music in Britain. These individuals were energised by a particular sense of folk culture that had been developing in Europe since the eighteenth century and which, as the Industrial Revolution gathered pace, became increasingly influential in a variety of social, political and cultural contexts. For many people working in many different countries, identifying and salvaging the music of 'the folk' became part of a crusade during the latter part of the nineteenth century – for it was there, in the music of the people (so they believed), that the soul of the nation resided.

Among the host of international names who contributed to this critical-editorial tradition, two stand out. Francis James Child (1825–96) was an American scholar based at Harvard University. After early career work on the poetic traditions of the Atlantic Archipelago, in the early 1870s Child commenced the research that would lead to the five-volume *English and Scottish Popular Ballads* (1882–98), which Roud calls 'the most important publication in the field, and effectively the founding document in serious ballad studies'. The other name to note is that of Cecil Sharp (1859–1924), whose energy, methods and single-minded vision of the field established him as the most influential folk song collector and editor of the twentieth century. Sharp's interest extended to maritime music, and in 1914 he published a book of 'English folk-chanteys', many of them collected from a retired sailor named John Short ('Yankee Jack') of Watchet in Somerset.

The shanty constituted a particular niche within the general folk project, attracting its own specialist collectors, many of whom had experience before the mast: Master Mariner W.B. Whall (1847–1917) joined the merchant navy aged 14 and spent ten years at sea; Sir Richard Runciman Terry (1865–1938) was the son of a sailor, and was deeply immersed in ocean lore from an early age; even the American collector Joanna Colcord (1882–1960) had extensive nautical experience, having been born at sea and spending much of her youth aboard ships captained by her father. The most influential collector of all, Stan Hugill (1906–92), is sometimes referred to as the last working shantyman, having served 23 years at sea, and experienced wrecks and capture by wartime enemies along the way.

This revival was, in my view, undertaken in the name of a 'folk' whose historical reality was questionable, and whose integrity was *invented* or *imposed* to a significant extent rather than *discovered*. This also accounts for the prevailing *declensionist* mode which suffuses folk research (including shanty research) – the sense that something of implicit value to the people is *being* lost, or *has been* lost, or is *about to be* lost, and that it's the researcher's duty to salvage the material traces (the songs) of a more deserving time (the past) and to preserve them as far as possible in their pristine state.

Experience and observation have convinced me that this is a forlorn hope; but that doesn't mean that we can't enjoy these powerful echoes from the past – in

different ways, certainly, and for different reasons, probably. If you're in any doubt of that mysterious power, find some friends and sing one of these songs – you'll soon discover what I mean.

'Mary Jane', sheet music, 1901.

# 6. BLOW THE MAN DOWN

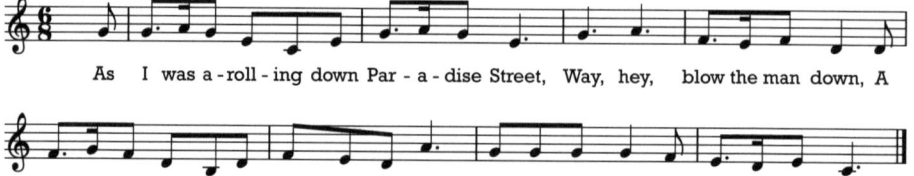

As I was a-rolling down Paradise Street, Way, hey, blow the man down, A big Irish copper I happened to meet, Give me some time to blow the man down

As I was a-rolling down Paradise Street
   *Way, hey, blow the man down*
A big Irish copper I happened to meet
   *Give me some time to blow the man down*

CHORUS:
Oh blow the man down, bullies, blow the man down
   *Timme way, hey, blow the man down*
Blow him right back to Liverpool town
   *Give me some time to blow the man down*

He said, 'You're a Black Baller by the cut of your hair
You're a Black Baller by the clothes that you wear'

I said to the scuffer 'You got me all wrong
I'm a flying-fish sailor just home from Hong Kong'

'No, you've sailed in some packet that flies the Black Ball
You've robbed some poor sailor of boots, clothes, and all'

Says he to me, 'Look, mate, you're breaking the law'
So I smashed in his face and I stove in his jaw

Well, they gave me six months in Liverpool town
For a-beating and a-kicking and a-blowing him down

A Liverpool ship and a Liverpool crew
A Liverpool mate and a Scouse skipper too

Red Jacket *engraving by Jacques La Grange, 1936.*

T his well-known halyard shanty came into its own during the period of the Western Ocean packet ships – roughly speaking, between about 1840 and 1870. The crews that worked these ships were commonly referred to as 'Packet Rats', and, as tends to happen in every specialised profession, they developed their own patois. In this case, it's clear that 'blow' signifies 'knock' or 'punch' or incapacitate in some manner. (John Short of Watchet, who was Cecil Sharp's main source, sang this shanty as 'Knock a Man Down'.) The word – indeed the song – clearly signals the violence that was part and parcel of the merchant mariner's life.

Stan Hugill traces the evolution of 'Blow the Man Down' through the stevedores of Mobile Bay and back to an African-American adaptation of an Irish-Scots melody. He also identifies six main versions, each with their own extended family of variations. Some of these are based in London, some involve milkmaids, some (as here) make reference to the infamous Black Ball Line (the narrator is a 'Black Baller'). The decidedly 'Rabelaisian' or bawdy nature of most precludes transcription. In this one, a 'flying-fish sailor' – which is to say, someone who plied his trade in Asiatic rather than Atlantic waters – drifts into the Liverpool Sailortown, only to fall foul of a 'scuffer' with no imagination and too much time on his hands.

'Blow the Man Down' is one of those shanties with a call-and-response chorus after each verse. 'Timme' is a stock phrase used in many shanties: a variation on 'to my' (as in 'here's to'), or 'to me' (as in 'listen to me' or 'rally to me' in martial discourse). Its principal function here is to cue the response.

*Right:* A Clipper Ship in a Hurricane, *lithograph by Currier & Ives, between 1856 and 1907.*

*Opposite:* A deck *view of a rolling ship,* Imperator Alexander, *between 1885 and 1920.*

# 7. BONEY WAS A WARRIOR

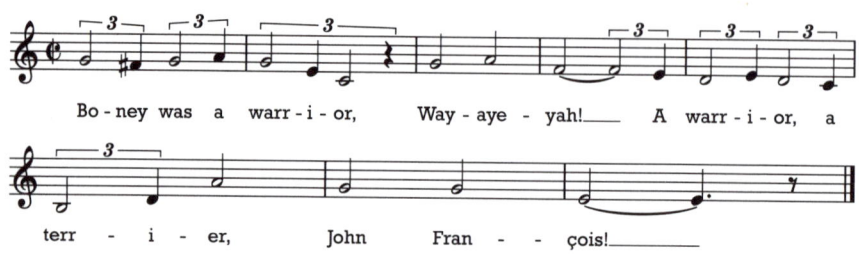

Boney was a warrior,
*Way-aye yah!*
A warrior, a terrier
*John François!*

Boney fought the Prussians
The Austrians, the Russians

Boney went to school in France
He learnt to make the Russians dance

Oh, Boney went to Moscow
All through the ice and snow

Moscow was a-blazing
And Boney was a-raging

Boney was a Frenchy-man
Then he had to turn again

Boney went to Elba
Wished he'd never been there

He beat the Prussians squarely
He beat the English nearly

'Twas on the plains of Waterloo
He met the boy who put him through

Boney went a-cruising
Aboard the Billy Ruffian

They sent him into exile
He died on Saint Helena's Isle

He was a rorty general
A rorty, snorty general

## O
r 'Bonny Was a Warrior', according to Laura Smith – a spelling repeated by Cecil Sharp (when he collected it at the beginning of the twentieth century from John Short) and then again by Richard Terry in his collection. 'Bonny' sounds strange to modern ears, for whom the Napoleonic nickname of 'Boney' is well established.

Terry also wondered at the once-great enemy's popularity among British seamen: was it empathy with his fate as a virtual maroon on the remote Atlantic island of St Helena, or a salute to a gallant enemy?

In any event, this shanty was a favourite on British ships long after the 'Great Terror' himself had died (although not the fear of invasion from the European mainland that he represented). There was in fact a degree of contemporary British support for revolutionary republicanism, and indeed for the 'rorty' (meaning boisterous or high-spirited) emperor himself. Hugill repeats Sampson's speculation that this song may in fact derive from a broadside ballad of the period. It's more likely, however, that it dates to a period when the threat had receded and Napoleon himself had metamorphosed from imminent menace to romantic hero. Whatever the song's original aspirations to accuracy (Napoleon was indeed imprisoned aboard the *Bellerephon* – the 'Billy Ruffian' referred to in the lyric – in Plymouth harbour after surrendering), its shanty career sent poor Boney on adventures far and wide, some involving false women, some (when adapted aboard American ships) even sending him across the Rocky Mountains!

Like most shanties, 'Boney' was versatile; but at least one of its applications was as a short haul, hand-over-hand shanty used to 'sweat up' – that is (as described by Proctor) 'to make the final tightening haul in order to get a good set on a sail'. With the hauling motion falling on the last syllables of the second and fourth lines ('yah' and 'çois' – usually pronounced 'swor'), it's a good shanty for novices to experience the power of the form, and to begin to appreciate the vital role played by this kind of music when trying to undertake onerous tasks in difficult conditions.

# 8. BULLY IN THE ALLEY

So help me bob, I'm bully in the alley
*Way aye, bully in the alley*
Help me bob, I'm bully in the alley
*Bully down in Shinbone Al*

Sally is a girl in Shinbone Alley
Sally is the girl that I spliced nearly

I found myself out on a spree-o
I found myself with time so free-o

I waltzed up to the Angel Inn-o
I kicked on the door and walked right in-o

I walked up to the barroom counter
There I met with Greasy Annie

I bought her rum and I bought her gin-o
I bought her wine of white and red-o

And when I'd spent of all my tin-o
Off to bed we both did creep-o

We rough-and-tumbled all night long-o
When dawn did break the cock did crow-o

I left my girl to go a-sailing
I left my Sal to go a-whaling

This is another of the shanties first collected by Cecil Sharp from John Short. Stan Hugill included a short version in his *Shanties from the Seven Seas*, claiming that it was a halyard shanty of African-American or Caribbean origin – based on the fact that there are 'Shinbone Alleys' in various ports scattered across the region. There are also reports that it was popular among the cotton hoosiers (or stowers) of the Gulf of Mexico ports.

The word 'bully' has different meanings in the shanty lexicon. Relating to the culture of violent intimidation that was rife at sea and onshore, it can mean a bully or to bully as most of us would understand the word. It can also mean 'headstrong and jolly' – as in 'my bully boys of Liverpool' (see No. 38). In this instance it just seems to mean paralytic drunk; and 'bully in the alley' might well refer to the practice of leaving an inebriated buddy somewhere safe to be collected at the end of an evening's revelries. 'So help me bob' was once a common idiom expressing surprise; heard somewhat differently, however – 'help me, Bob, I'm incapacitated in this alleyway, likely to get robbed or perhaps killed unless you lend me your assistance' – we might say that everyone has need of a 'Bob' in their life at some stage!

The 'Sally' verses at the top and tail of this shanty seem somewhat out of place in the context of the usual sailor-meets-girl format. Of course, 'Sally' was an established figure within the shanty pantheon (see No. 30); but there has also been some speculation that she may in this instance have strayed in from 'Sally in Our Alley', a popular eighteenth-century English song written by Henry Carey that was popular aboard Royal Navy ships in the latter decades of the nineteenth century, as reported, for example, in Sam Noble's memoir *'Tween Decks in the Seventies*.

'Bully in the Alley' is unusual in that besides the traditional solo-refrain structure of the verses, it starts with a chorus, which is then repeated after every verse. Despite its problematic provenance and somewhat odd structure, it's a truly rousing shanty, and great fun to sing.

British Grog, *by John Frederick Herring Junior, 1831*

# 9. CAN'T YOU DANCE THE POLKA?

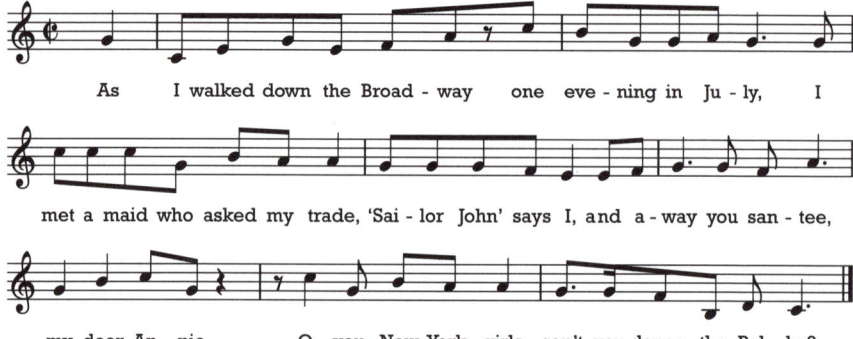

As I walked down the Broadway one evening in July
I met a maid who asked my trade, 'Sailor John' says I
    And away you santee, my dear Annie
    O you New York girls, can't you dance the Polka?

To Tiffany's I took her, not caring about expense
I bought her two gold earrings, they cost me fifteen cents

Says she, 'You Limejuice sailor, now see me home you may'
But when we reached her cottage door unto me she did say

'My flash man he's a Yankee with his hair cut short behind
He wears a tarry jumper, sails in the Black Ball Line.'

'He's homeward bound this evening and with me he will stay
So get a move-on sailor-boy, get cracking on your way'

So I kissed her hard and proper before that flash man came.
'Oh fare thee well, my Bowery girl, I know your little game!'

I wrapped my glad-rags round me and to the docks did steer
I'll never court another maid, I'll stick to rum and beer

I joined a Yankee blood-boat and sailed away next morn
Don't ever fool around with girls, you're safer off Cape Horn

Described by Richard Terry as 'a prime favourite' on both British and American vessels, an early version of this capstan shanty was known as 'Away, Susanna'. Stan Hugill speculates that its melody was adapted from an Irish ballad named 'Larry Doolin' (also known as 'The Irish Jaunting Car'), and links it with the 'polkamania' that swept Europe and the United States in the middle decades of the nineteenth century. He also tells us that the original words were unprintable.

It may be that the word 'Santee' featuring in close proximity to 'Annie' suggests a reference to 'Santiana' – the Mexican general who has his own shanty (No. 31). In any event, this is a good example of the 'port' song, warning of the dangers of high hopes and pretty girls. The narrator here just about escapes getting turned over (see 'Sailortown'), although why he joins 'a Yankee blood-boat' – a ship on which brutality was the norm – remains unclear. The shanty is not the place to look for coherence or consistency.

This shanty is also widely known as 'New York Girls'. In Martin Scorsese's 2002 film *Gangs of New York*, which is set largely in the Bowery and Five Points slum districts of New York in the early years of the American Civil War, the Irish traditional musician Finbar Furey sings the version included by the influential American collector William Doerflinger in his *Shantymen and Shantyboys* (1951). All these Irish connections are indicative of the extent to which that country's expansive musical heritage contributed to the nineteenth-century shanty tradition.

*Detail from a print relating to the first night of the Amsterdam Fair, 1857.*

# 10. CHEER'LY MAN

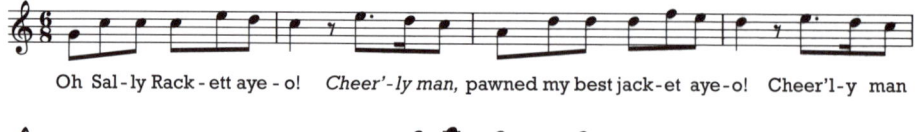

Oh Sally Rackett aye-o!
*Cheer'ly man*
Pawned my best jacket aye-o!
*Cheer'ly man*
And kept the ticket aye-o!
Cheery aye-o! Hauley aye-o!
*Cheer'ly man*

Oh Nancy Dawson aye-o!
She's got a notion aye-o!
For our old bo'sun aye-o!
Cheery aye-o! Hauley aye-o!

Oh Betsy Baker aye-o!
Lived in Long Acre aye-o!
Married a Quaker aye-o!
Cheery aye-o! Hauley aye-o!

Oh ladies of the town aye-o!
All soft as down aye-o!
In their best gown aye-o!
Cheery aye-o! Hauley aye-o!

Oh Polly Hawkins aye-o!
With her white stockings aye-o!
Beats all at talking aye-o!
Cheery aye-o! Hauley aye-o!

Oh Kitty Carson aye-o!
Jilted the parson aye-o!
Married a mason aye-o!
Cheery aye-o! Hauley aye-o!

Oh haughty cocks aye-o!
Oh split the blocks aye-o!
Oh stretch her luff aye-o!
Cheery aye-o! Hauley aye-o!

Oh rouse and shake her aye-o!
Oh shake and wake her aye-o!
Oh go we'll wake her aye-o!
Cheery aye-o! Hauley aye-o!

ack in 1888, Laura Smith remembered this as a shanty named 'Sally Racket', latterly obsolete but once very popular among sailors loading timber in Quebec. She claimed that its likely musical origins lay in the songs sung by African-Americans 'stowing cotton in the holds of ships in Southern ports'. She also noted that while the response lines remain the same throughout, the uneven length of the solo lines required some creative phrasing from the shantyman. Richard Terry attempted to accommodate the shanty's wayward structure within an unlikely 9/8 time signature, and a piano introduction to be played 'a la Chopin'! Bert Lloyd sang a version with a 'Haul 'im away' response on the album *Sailors' Songs & Sea Shanties* (1957).

Stan Hugill described 'Cheer'ly Man' as a rudimentary halyard shanty – hardly a song at all, in fact, more a series of (largely unprintable) shouts, calls and grunts. For this reason he describes it as 'probably the most primitive, and one of the oldest of all these heaving and hauling songs of the sea' – an opinion that derived (via Cecil Sharp) from John Short. Hugill also notes that the word 'cheer'ly' (sometimes pronounced 'cheer-i-lie') most frequently meant 'quickly' (as employed by the boatswain in Shakespeare's *The Tempest*: 'Heigh, my hearts! Cheerly, cheerly, my hearts!'), although just to complicate matters there's an alternative Royal Navy usage meaning 'slow and steady'! This latter form is interesting, insofar as 'Cheer'ly Man' was (according to the Anglo-Australian singer and historian Danny Spooner) 'one of only two shanties allowed to be sung aboard Royal Navy vessels' where it was used for raising – slowly and steadily, no doubt – the anchor.

Another interesting word used in this shanty is the multi-functional 'luff', which (as noun, verb and adjective) relates to the practice of sailing close to the wind in order to gain speed.

# 11. CLEAR THE TRACK, LET THE BULLGINE RUN

Oh the smart-est pack-et that you could find, Ah - hey, ah - ho, are you 'most done? is the

old *Wild Cat* of the Swal-low-tail Line, clear the track and let the bull-gine run, tim - me

hey rig-a-jin in a jaunt-ing car, ah - hey, ah - ho, are you 'most done? E -

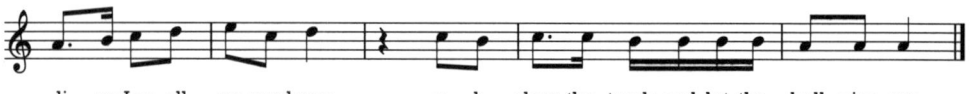

- li - za Lee all on my knee, o - h clear the track and let the bull-gine run

Oh the smartest packet that you could find
*Ah-hey, ah-ho, are you 'most done?*
Is the old *Wild Cat* of the Swallowtail Line
*Clear the track and let the bullgine run*
Timme hey rig-a-jin in a jaunting car
*Ah hey, ah-ho, are you 'most done?*
Eliza Lee all on my knee ... oh
*Clear the track and let the bullgine run*

Oh the old *Wild Cat* of the Swallowtail Line
She's never a day behind her time

Oh we're outward bound for New York Town
Them Bowery girls we'll waltz around

When we've stowed our freight at the West Street Pier
We'll be homeward bound to our Liverpool beer

Oh wake her, shake her afore we're done
Wake that girl with the blue dress on

When we all gets back to Liverpool town
I'll stand you whiskies all around

And when I'm home again from sea
Eliza, won't you marry me?

**W.B.** Whall cites a version of this capstan shanty as a minstrel ditty full of comic biblical references, claiming that 'the words and tune of the first part were taken straight from the music hall'. Most other collectors prefer the one in which the glories of one or another of the American flash packets – their fancy, fast clippers – are celebrated. Laura Smith's early version has 'the Margret Evans, in the Black Cross Line'; Cecil Sharp had it as 'the Marg'ret Evans of the Blue Cross Line' – this was the version, incidentally, learned by the Irish writer James Joyce, and subsequently incorporated into his great novel *Ulysses*; Richard Terry gives us 'the Marget [sic] Evans of the Blue Cross Line', while John Sampson has it as 'the Marg'ret Evans of the Blue Star Line'. 'The old "Wild Cat" of the Swallow Tail Line' is Stan Hugill's variation, however, and he also has the most intriguing theory as to this shanty's genealogy.

'Clear The Track' has its origins on the American railroad ('bullgine' was American slang for a railway engine), where it was sung both to co-ordinate and to ease the backbreaking work – just as shanties were sung aboard ships. Hugill claims that the tune was adapted from the ancient Irish song 'Siubhail A Gradh' (pronounced *Shule Agraw*), which fetched up in Mobile Bay (in the state of Alabama) sometime during the Great Famine emigration of the 1840s. (The influence of that particular song's modal melody may also be heard, Sharp claims, in shanties such as 'Santiana' and 'Whip Jamboree'.)

One can easily imagine a scenario whereby an attractive melody – with perhaps incomprehensible Gaelic lyrics – is heard and adapted by the crew aboard one of those great floating villages. A version developed by African-American and Irish railroad gangs eventually made its way back to the port of Mobile where it was picked up by American and British crews plying the coastal and Atlantic trade routes. The adaptation of the lyrics for a variation on the 'flash packet' genre had transformed a Gaelic love song into an Anglo-American shanty.

Sailor in the Rigging, *watercolour by Herman Heijenbrock, 1904.*

# Music and the Sea

The sea is an elemental fact of life on this planet, figuring deeply within what the psychologist Carl Jung referred to as the collective human unconscious. Besides its practical uses (in which context it has contributed centrally to the development of human civilisation in areas such as trade, exploration and warfare), the sea has been an object of (or perhaps a space for) artistic endeavour for millennia – at least since the end of the last ice age (ca. 10,000 BCE).

It may be because of its primal nature that the sea has featured strongly in our most ubiquitous cultural form. Before humans were drawing on cave walls, long before they were developing the written forms which would enable them to develop complex stories, they were using the body's musical resources to communicate and to articulate meaning. Humming, clapping, whistling, manipulating pitch, imitating natural sound, and eventually singing – many anthropologists are convinced that these are the abilities which drove the early evolution of our species with its unique network of interconnected physical and neurological abilities.

For musical artists in the nineteenth century, perhaps *because* of its role in what would come to be described as 'folk music', the sea functioned as a powerful image of perennial human experience in a world undergoing rapid change. This interest extended from opera (with quasi-naturalistic settings and themes) to 'programme' music (music composed with a view to *suggesting* or *replicating* oceanic effects) to song-settings of poetry with nautical themes.

For example, the sea operates as a potent symbol of human struggle in *The Flying Dutchman* (1843), a story about a haunted ship in which Richard Wagner tried out some of the techniques which in later works would establish him as probably the most influential artist of the century. Wagner's 'ghost' haunts important twentieth-century English works such as Benjamin Britten's *Peter Grimes* (1945, whose 'sea interludes' are often performed as separate pieces) and *Billy Budd* (1951), based on Herman Melville's posthumously published novel.

One influential strand of 'sea music' is represented by Felix Mendelssohn in the works *Calm Sea and Prosperous Voyage* (1828) and *The Hebrides (Fingal's Cave)* (1833). Edward Elgar's five-song cycle *Sea Pictures* (1899) is implicated in the late-Victorian romanticism which inspired the early shanty collectors, while the same 'classical' fascination with the sea informs the work of a triumvirate of twentieth-century French composers: Albert Roussel, Antoine Mariotte and Jean Cras.

Around the turn of the twentieth century, two other French composers attempted modernist reappraisals of the sea-music tradition. In 'A Boat on the Ocean', the third movement of *Mirrors* piano suite first performed in 1906, Maurice Ravel deployed complex arpeggios and sweeping melodies to suggest the movement of the ocean. Claude Debussy's *The Sea* (1903–05) was subtitled *Three Symphonic Sketches for Orchestra*, and represents perhaps the culmination of art music's attempt to encapsulate (rather than merely to *represent*) the sea's mysterious power. This latter work was also a clear influence on Jan Sibelius's tone poem *The Oceanides*, first performed in 1914.

It's a long way from 'Across the Western Ocean' to *The Oceanides*, from the rigours of working-class struggle to the essentially middle-class pleasures of the concert hall. It's interesting to consider that these responses may be locked into the same basic endeavour – the one focusing on the sea as a measure of our perennial humanity.

Chrysolite, *engraving by Jacques La Grange, 1936.*

# 12. THE DEAD HORSE

They say, old man, your horse will die
*And they say so, and we hope so*
They say, old man, your horse will die
*Oh poor old man!*

And if he dies then we'll tan his hide
And if he lives then we'll ride him again

For one long month I rode him hard
For one long month we rode him hard

One month a hell-bent life we've led
While you laid up in a nice warm bed

But now your month is up, Old Turk
Get up, you swine, and look for work

After many years with much abuse
We'll salt him down for sailors' use

He's as dead as a nail in the lamp room floor
And he won't bother us no more

We'll hoist him up to the main yard-arm
And drop him down to the depths of the sea

We'll sink him down with a long, long roll
Where the sharks'll have his body and the
    devil his soul

sailors were usually paid a month in advance. Some dutifully passed the money along to wives; some used it to acquire the necessities (all those items not supplied by their employers) for an arduous sea voyage; some squandered it or were swindled out of it in Sailortown. In any event, this meant that the men were effectively working for nothing during the first month at sea. Once they began to earn again, 'the dead horse' of debt could be dispatched. Captain Whall described it thus:

*[On] the last evening of the month, at one bell in the second dog-watch, a lighted procession emerged from the break of the forecastle, a wheeled platform carried the rude figure of a horse made of canvas stuffed with straw, upon which sat one of the boatswain's mates in old clothes and a battered tall hat, waving a long whip. He was dragged along by the men who sang as they dragged ... On reaching the quarter-deck, the rider dismounted and addressed his steed ... This address ended, the figure was run up to the lee main yardarm, where a man was ready with a blue light and a knife. Having fired the blue light, he cut away the steed, which fell into the water to the hurrahs of the crew.*

Whall also says that 'The Dead Horse' was ceremonial only, but others (including John Sampson and Stan Hugill) disagree, claiming it was used at halyards even after the practice described above was discontinued. Typical 'working' verses would normally be appended for this kind of usage: 'I thought I heard the old man say/ And they say so, and we hope so/It's time for us to roll and go/Oh poor old man'. 'And as we sail around Cape Horn/And they say so, and we hope so/Well you'll wish to God you'd never been born/Oh poor old man'. And so on.

The version included here is a combination of the one provided by Hugill and the one recorded as 'Poor Old Horse' by The Albion Band for their classic album *Rise Up Like the Sun* (1978) – although omitting the bawdy verses their version borrowed from 'The Hog-Eye Man' (No. 19).

*Detail from a print relating to the first night of the Amsterdam Fair, 1857.*

# 13. DRUNKEN SAILOR

What shall we do with a drunk-en sai-lor, what shall we do with a drunk-en sai-lor,

What shall we do with a drunk-en sai - lor ear - lie in the morn - ing?

What shall we do with a drunken sailor?
*What shall we do with a drunken sailor?*
What shall we do with a drunken sailor
*Ear-lie in the morning?*

CHORUS:
*Hoorah and up she rises*
*Hoorah and up she rises*
*Hoorah and up she rises*
*Ear-lie in the morning*

Put him in the longboat and make him bale her (× 3)

Put him in the bilge and make him drink it (× 3)

Put him in the scuppers with a hose-pipe on him (× 3)

Shave his chest with a rusty razor (× 3)

Put him in the guard room till he gets sober (× 3)

The Lads of the Ocean,
*print by Isaac & George*
*Cruikshank, 1805.*

The melody of this famous shanty is that of an ancient Irish clan march named 'Oró sé do bheatha 'bhaile', roughly translating as 'Hurrah, Welcome Home!' The 'early' in one of its alternative titles is invariably pronounced 'earl-lie', and its popularity outside nautical circles may derive from its use in schools as part of a music education programme. Bawdy versions have been adapted in a wide range of male-dominated environments since the early nineteenth century.

According to Captain Whall, it was one of only two shanties (the other being 'Cheer'ly Man') allowed in the Royal Navy, where it was used as a 'stamp-and-go'. Also known as a 'walk-away' or 'runaway', this form of work song (as described by David Proctor) required a line of sailors to turn 'their backs to the fall and the shantyman, and [stamp] with their feet to keep the rhythm going as they hauled on the rope.' Whall was surely wrong, however, in asserting that this shanty had only *two* verses, when research has in fact uncovered a large number of punishments for this particular inebriated mariner.

Some of these scenarios – drinking bilge water, for example, or having one's private parts shaved – are comic and grotesque. Behind the comedy, however, lies a reality that obtained both in the merchant service and in the Royal Navy; a reality driving the mutually supporting energies of capitalism and militarism; a reality comprised of strict discipline, on the one hand, and opportunistic resistance on the other. Why is the sailor drunk? Who devised and enforced the cruel and unusual punishments to which he is subjected? When he comes to a sense of himself, hungover in that guard room, will he be chastened or incensed?

# 14. FIRE DOWN BELOW

Fire in the galley, fire in the house
Fire in the beef-kid, scorching all the scouse
  *Fire, fire, fire down below*
  *Fetch a bucket of water, girls, there's fire down*
  *below*

Fire in the fore-peak, fire down below
Fire in the fore-chains, the bosun doesn't know

Fire in the lifeboat, fire in the gig
Fire in the pigsty roasting the pig

Fire in the lower-hold, fire down below
Fire in the main-well, the Captain doesn't know

Fire up aloft, me boys, fire all aglow
Fire in the galley, the cook he doesn't know

Fire on the royal yard, fire on the main
Fetch a bucket of water, girls, put it out again

Fire at the capstan, fire at the mast
Fire on the main-deck, and she's burning fast

Fire in the storeroom, burning all the food
Fire at the knightheads, burning all the wood

Fire up above, me boys, fire down below
Douse it out with water, girls, and let us roll and go

The prospect of fire at sea was obviously a source of worry in wooden vessels, even after the introduction of iron and steel frames. The 'fire ship' – a vessel filled with combustible materials, deliberately set aflame and steered into the ranks of the enemy – had been an established part of maritime warfare since ancient times. In the famous crisis of 1588, Sir Francis Drake used this tactic against the ships of the Spanish Armada.

The shanties invariably refer to a different kind of 'fire', however: the pain, advancing (if untreated) to the point of incapacity and death, of syphilis. Sexually transmitted diseases were rife in all walks of life before the development of modern treatments; indeed, there's a well-established cultural theory linking nineteenth-century Romantic inspiration with the heightened mental states consequent upon syphilitic infection. It's a rum thought – that so much of what we consider the basis of modern Western civilisation, from Beethoven to Nietzsche, from Byron to Wilde, may actually be the product of the diseased imagination.

As may be imagined, sailors were particularly vulnerable to infections of this nature. During the sixteenth and seventeenth centuries, 'fire-ship' became a generic term for a diseased prostitute, and there are numerous ballads dedicated to an exposition of the same fatal story – the one in which Jack rocks into port with his pay, looking for entertainment, only to encounter a 'fire-ship' whose apparent attractions lead him to suppress his common sense. James Hanley's novel *Boy* (1931) offers a grim variation on this tale: a 13-year-old cabin boy from Liverpool is euthanised by his captain after contracting syphilis in an Egyptian brothel.

Because this shanty was sung at pumps (which was a long job) there tended to be many verses, and the limited incendiary opportunities aboard the average wooden ship would no doubt have tested the shantyman's ingenuity. Stan Hugill recalled singing a version of 'Fire Down Below' while pumping the four-masted *Garthpoole* shortly before it was wrecked on a reef near the Cape Verde Islands in October 1929.

# 15. GOODBYE, FARE-YE-WELL

Oh, don't you he-ar the Ol-d Man say, Good-bye, fare-ye-well, good-bye fare-ye-well, Oh,

do-n't you he-ar the Ol-d Man say, Hur-rah, me boys, we're ho-me-ward bound

Oh, don't you hear the Old Man say
   *Goodbye, fare-ye-well, goodbye fare-ye-well*
Oh, don't you hear the Old Man say
   *Hurrah, me boys, we're homeward bound*

We're homeward bound for old Liverpool town
Where all of them Judies are hanging around

And when we get back to the Wallasey Gates
Sally and Polly for their flash men do wait

And one to another you'll hear them all say
Oh here comes young Jack with his fourteen months pay

Them gals there on Lime Street we soon hope to meet
And soon we'll be rolling both sides of the street

We're homeward bound for the girls of the town
So stamp up my hearties, and heave her around

We'll meet these fly Judies and ring the old bell
With the girls that we meet there we'll raise bloody hell

I'll tell my old woman when I get back home
Them flash girls on Lime Street won't leave me alone

We're homeward bound to the girls of the town
So heave away bullies, we're all homeward bound

We're homeward bound and I'll have you to know
It's over the water to Liverpool we'll go

**T**his was a popular homeward-bound shanty sung at the capstan while raising anchor; in fact, Captain Whall's version even contains a reference to a spinning capstan, which he reckons dates it to a time before the introduction of the brake windlass around the middle of the nineteenth century. As usual, there are multiple versions (including some coarse ones, *pace* Richard Terry), as this shanty was regularly 'mashed' with material from 'The *Dreadnought*', 'Homeward Bound', 'Blow the Man Down' and 'The Mermaid'.

The destination port might change from ship to ship and shipping line to shipping line – London, Portsmouth, New York, and so forth – but 'Goodbye, Fare-Ye-Well' is another of those quintessential Liverpool shanties. I wrote in the introduction about the way in which a particular geographical location can accumulate a resonance in the minds of those who may have never actually been there. Just so in this song: the place-names, the personalities, the 'mood' of the city – it's all there. In some senses, in fact, nineteenth-century Liverpool fulfilled the role that places such as New York, London and Paris did in the twentieth – which is to say: it was as much a shared international cultural 'idea' as a real place.

In transcribing her version, Laura Smith employed a musical instruction that I have never before encountered: *affettuoso* – translating as 'affectionately'. What does it mean to sing a song 'affectionately'? Shanties provided the soundtrack to a difficult way of life in a difficult world – more difficult than we, with our welfare safety net, can perhaps imagine. Perhaps we should be reassured by the presence of positive human emotions – empathy, affection, even love – among all that hardship, violence and grief.

A Famed Smuggler, Will Watch, Kissed His Sue, illustration by V. Whall, 1910.

# 16. HANGING JOHNNY

Oh they call me Hang-ing John-ny, A-way, bo-ys, a-way, They say I hang for mon-ey, so hang, boys, hang

>  Oh they call me Hanging Johnny
>  *Away, boys, away*
>  They say I hang for money
>  *So hang, boys, hang*

They say I hang for money
But hanging is so funny

At first I hanged my daddy
And then I hanged me mammy

Yes, I hanged me dear old mother
My sister and me brother

I hanged my sister Sally
I hanged the whole damn family

And then I hanged me granny
I strung her up quite canny

I'd hang the mate and skipper
I'd hang them by their flippers

I'd hang a ruddy copper
I'd give him the long dropper

I'd hang a rotten liar
I'd hang a blooming friar

I'd hang to make things jolly
I'd hang Jill, Jane and Polly

A rope, a beam, a ladder
I'd hang yiz all together

We'll hang and haul together
We'll hang for better weather

*Unbending a foretopsail and sending it down, on the* Loch Etive, *between 1885 and 1914.*

T his cheery riot of gore', as Richard Terry points out, 'is wedded to the most plaintive of tunes'. In his useful book *A Sailor's Garland* (1906), the poet John Masefield (who loved all things nautical) described the melody of 'Hanging Johnny' as one of the saddest things he had ever encountered. He goes on:

*I heard it for the first time off the Horn in a snowstorm, when we were hoisting topsails after heavy weather. There was a heavy, grey sea running and the decks were awash. The skies were sodden and oily, shutting in the sea about a quarter of a mile away. Some birds were flying about us, screaming ... I thought at the time that it was the whole scene set to music. I cannot repeat those words to their melancholy wavering music without seeing the line of yellow oilskins, the wet deck, the frozen ropes, and the great grey seas running up into the sky.*

Some believe the eponymous hero of this halyard shanty was the seventeenth-century executioner John ('Jack') Ketch, whose victims included Lord Russell and the Duke of Monmouth, and whose defective technique made his name a byword for gory death.

'Hanging Johnny' was sung in London in 1926 as accompaniment to the film *The Sea Beast* (1926), a version of *Moby Dick* featuring the silent screen star John Barrymore. In the notes to his collection published the following year, John Sampson decried the speed with which it had been sung by ignorant 'landsmen' on that occasion, although a quicker, shorter version was in fact often used for 'sweating up' – the final haul to ensure that a sail was set as tightly and as efficiently as possible.

# 17. HAUL AWAY, JOE

When I was just a lit-tle lad, and so me mo-ther told me, a-way, haul a-way,— we'll haul a-way, Joe— That if I did-n't kiss the girls me lips would get all moul-dy, a- -way, haul a-way,— we'll haul a-wa-ay, Joe— A-way, haul a-way, we'll haul a-way to-ge-ther, a-way, haul a-way,— we'll haul a-wa-ay, Joe

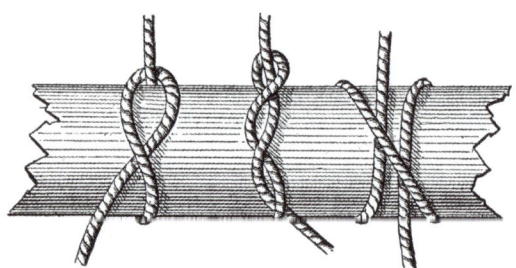

When I was just a little lad, and so me mother told me
　　*Away, haul away, we'll haul away, Joe*
That if I didn't kiss the girls me lips would get all mouldy
　　*Away, haul away, we'll haul away, Joe*
Away, haul away, we'll haul away together
　　*Away, haul away, we'll haul away, Joe*

Talk about your Yankee girls and up-in-corner-Sallies
But they couldn't make the grade with the girls from Booble Alley

King Louis was the King of France before the revolution
But the people cut his head off and it spoilt his constitution

Saint Patrick was a gentleman, he came of decent people
He built a church in Dublin town and on it set a steeple

Once I had a Chinese girl as sweet as sugar candy
I lost her to a Portugee all dressed up like a dandy

Well then I had a German girl and she was fat and lazy
But then I got a Yankee girl who damn-near drove me crazy

Once I had an Irish girl, her name was Nellie Flanagan
She stole my boots, she stole my plate, she stole my cash
　　and pannikin

Hey, can't you see the black cloud a-rising?
Hey, can't you see the black cloud a-rising?

I thought I heard the old man say it's time for us to roll and go
So now we're leaving Liverpool bound for the bay of Mexico

　　*Away, haul away, we'll hope for better weather*
　　*Away, haul away, we'll haul away Joe*

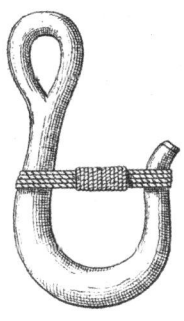

There exists a whole family of songs focused on the activity of hauling, which, as has been shown, was one of the principal shipboard tasks required of the nineteenth-century merchant mariner. 'Haul Away, Joe' belongs to this clan, although opinion is divided as to the precise hauling activity for which it was used. We remember again that 'versatility' was a useful attribute for any shanty. The multitude of available verses form a large reservoir of musical and lyrical images clustered around the same 'hauling' root.

In Chapter 22 of Herman Melville's *Moby Dick* (1851), the sailors sing a bawdy song about the girls of 'Booble Alley' as they are leaving the port of Nantucket; while in Chapter 39 of his earlier autobiographical novel, *Redburn: His First Voyage* (1849), based in part on a visit to Liverpool in 1839, Melville describes an encounter with a former sailor who tries to sell him a ballad that he has composed about a recent portside murder. Redburn's response typifies the prevailing impression of Sailortown held by all 'decent people':

*The pestilent lanes and alleys which, in their vocabulary, go by the names of Rotten-row, Gibraltar-place, and Booble-alley, are putrid with vice and crime; to which, perhaps, the round globe does not furnish a parallel ... These are the haunts from which sailors sometimes disappear forever; or issue in the morning, robbed naked, from the broken door-ways. These are the haunts in which cursing, gambling, pickpocketing, and common iniquities, are virtues too lofty for the infected gorgons and hydras to practice. Propriety forbids that I should enter into details; but kidnappers, burkers, and resurrectionists are almost saints and angels to them. They seem leagued together, a company of miscreant misanthropes, bent upon doing all the malice to mankind in their power. With sulphur and brimstone they ought to be burned out of their arches like vermin.*

Such a description (by arguably the greatest writer on the sea) speaks to the constant threat underscoring even such benign songs as 'Haul Away, Joe'. The weather may be set fair, but the black clouds are never too far away.

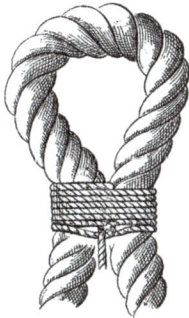

Pits and Pitmen – Coal Whipping in the Pool, *illustration from* The Graphic, *25 February, 1871.*

# Themes and Dreams

In terms of the characteristic themes of the shanty, it's difficult to generalise because lyrics tended to be occasional and improvised. The more physically demanding the shipboard task, the less sense required; 'songs' could descend into (just as they had in some cases emerged from) a series of grunts and nonsense images – some of them borrowed from 'foreign' languages such as Gaelic. Longer, more tedious tasks, on the other hand, could afford to be more expansive (both in structural and in lyrical terms) in order to engage the sailor's attention as well as his effort. There's plenty of evidence that some of the heartier narrative folk songs were adapted specifically for work gang purposes.

As will be clear from the commentaries, shanties may survive in many different versions, each of which can in turn have numerous variations.[4] Even now, when they are sung for entertainment rather than as an aid to work, performance will reflect the style and the predilections of the singers who, for whatever reason, will prefer *this* rather than *that* version, *this* rather than *that* variation. The characteristic line length and phrasing pattern allowed for a good deal of borrowing between shanties – something also facilitated by the existence of a sizeable stock of 'floating' formulations (references to particular ports, officer types, food quality, women's names, and so on) which could be readily adapted for any task at any time. All of this makes the identification and categorisation of shanties extremely challenging.

One dominant strain that my own research has revealed, however, concerns a kind of elemental dialogue between the ocean and the port – between *travelling* and *arriving*. Ocean songs long for land, and the port songs (even when they won't acknowledge it) long for the open sea; each, moreover, inheres in the other. In a shanty such as 'Whip Jamboree' (No. 39), for example, we witness the sailor plotting his eastward voyage towards Liverpool with growing excitement, watching out for landmarks (Cape Clear, Holyhead, Fort Perch Rock, Waterloo Dock) which signal his increasing proximity to the port, and preparing himself and his possessions for leaving the ship. The prospect of going ashore to sink a pint of beer while enjoying the entertainment in Dan Lowrey's famous music hall is eagerly anticipated.[5] After the initial pleasure of arrival, however, after the hangover kicks in and financial demands hove blurrily into view (see 'Sailortown'), the sailor has to face up to the prospect of going to sea once more. This will be a difficult and demanding undertaking, he knows – each trip is more difficult and demanding than the last until finally the prospect becomes too daunting and he settles down (if lucky) to a life onshore. But while he's still able, and despite the hardships and dangers of shipboard life, there remains something compelling about the prospect of a return to sea.

No doubt such romantic notions are largely the invention of bookish landlubbers such as myself but the evidence of the shanties suggests that while the port can service the sailor's need for physical stimulation, the ocean speaks to deeper longings – subconscious, unformulated, primordial.

*'The Sailor's Dream', by John Pridham, 1899.*

# 18. HAUL ON THE BOWLINE

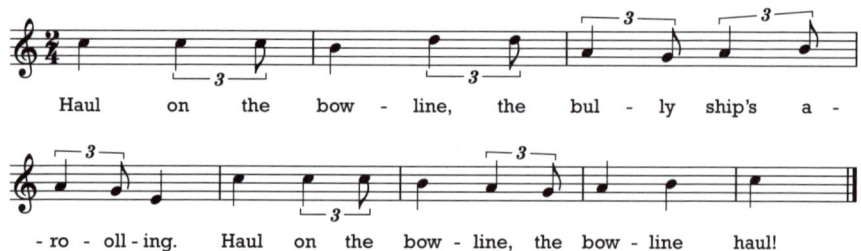

Haul on the bowline, the bully ship's a-rolling
*Haul on the bowline, the bowline haul!*

Haul on the bowline, the Old Man he's a growling

Haul on the bowline, the wind it is a-howling

Haul on the bowline, Kitty is my darling

Haul on the bowline, Kitty comes from Liverpool

Haul on the bowline, Liverpool's a fine town

Haul on the bowline, so early in the morning

Haul on the bowline, before the day was dawning

Haul on the bowline, we'll either break or bend it

Haul on the bowline, we're men enough to mend it

Haul on the bowline, it's a far cry to payday

Haul on the bowline, it's a long way to Liverpool

This is an unusual shanty inasmuch as it is named for, and quotes throughout, the activity for which it was used – hauling the bowline. That said, its title remains (as with so many of these songs) an issue and a range of alternatives exist[6] – all evidence, if more were needed, of the shanty's resistance to the hegemony of 'the final text'.

Whichever title is favoured, this shanty's primary use was to pull the sheets (ropes, wires of chains connected to the bottom corners of the sails) into their most efficient place. It's clearly a member of the great 'hauling' family of shanties – indeed, Hugill reckons it

could be the granddaddy of them all, seeing as how the 'bowline' was in use in medieval times, and probably much earlier. Its original function became rarer as ship design changed and the 'bowline' itself moved towards obsolescence, although the shanty was still being used for various hauling tasks right up until the end of the days of sail. (Another version was sung at the capstan.)

When used as a work song, the actual pull would come on the word 'haul' at the end of each verse, and this tends to work best when shouted rather than sung.

When performed in a non-work environment, some singers like to overlap the last 'haul' of the chorus with the first 'haul' of the next verse. Although this sounds unwieldy and rushed to me, we find this practice on one of the more interesting versions of 'Haul on the Bowline' recorded over the years – that by the legendary American folk-blues singer Dave van Ronk, who was the model for the eponymous hero of the Coen Brothers' 2013 film *Inside Llewyn Davis*.

The London Pool,
*illustration by Gustave Doré from* London: A Pilgrimage, *1872.*

# 19. THE HOG-EYE MAN

*Hand me down my rid-ing cane, I'm off to see my dar-ling Jane, and a hog-eye, Rail-road nav-vie with his hog-eye, Stead-y on a jig with a hog-eye-o, She wants the hog-eye man*

Hand me down my riding cane
I'm off to see my darling Jane, and a hog-eye
*Railroad navvie with his hog-eye*
*Steady on a jig with a hog-eye-o*
*She wants the hog-eye man*

Oh the hog-eye man is the man for me
Sailing down from Wallasey

He came to the shack where Sally did dwell
He knocked on the door, and he rang her bell

Now, it's 'Who's been here since I been gone?'
A railroad navvie with his seaboots on

If I catch him here with Sally once more
I'll sling me hook, go to sea once more

O Sally's in the garden sifting sand
And the hog-eye man sitting hand-in-hand

O Sally in the garden picking peas
Her golden hair hanging down to her knees

Oh the hog-eye man is the man for me
For he is blind and he can't see

O a hog-eye ship and a hog-eye crew
A hog-eye mate and a skipper too

**W.B.** Whall includes an elaborate gloss on this long-drag and capstan shanty, involving the California Gold Rush, railroad construction and a particular type of maritime vessel called a 'hog-eye'. However, according to Douglas Morgan, author of *Unexpurgated Sea Shanties*, 'hog-eye' was in fact 'a slang term for the female genitalia'. Variants of the term were used in a number of occupational contexts (including maritime and railroad), but it's the sexual connotation that has prevailed.

Richard Terry refers to 'Hog's-eye Man' and agrees with Whall that few of its infinite verses (accumulated through use by railroad navvies, rivermen, stevedores and deep-water sailors) were printable in their original form. Stan Hugill describes it as 'a shanty usually spoken of in hushed tones by collectors', admitting that 'the solo parts *were* indecent, and a large amount of camouflaging was necessary before this song could be made public'. In those other versions of the shanty, the presence of language that is now socially unacceptable raises the issue of how to engage with material that is highly offensive and categorically unusable (see 'Bawdy').[7]

The song seems to dramatise a stand-off between the competing attractions of the land and the sea. It remains unclear why 'darling Jane', invoked in the first verse, is discarded for the Sally who features throughout the rest of the song. Note the use of the nautical idiom 'sling me hook'; the reference is to the raising of the anchor into its housing 'sling', but the common meaning is to make oneself scarce. All these issues shouldn't detract from the interesting fact that 'The Hog-Eye Man' is one of a limited number of minor-key shanties, transposed, in all likelihood, from an earlier modal tune of African-American origin.

Miss Kitty & the Bag, illustration by George Cruikshank, from Charles Dibden's Songs Naval and National, *1841*.

# 20. JOHN KANAKA

I thought I heard the Old Man say, John Kan-a-ka-na-ka, too-rye-a, To-

-day, to-day's a hol-i-day, John Kan-a-ka-na-ka, too-rye-a,

Too-rye-a, ooh! too-tye-a, John Kan-a-ka-na-ka, too-rye-a

I thought I heard the Old Man say
*John Kanaka-naka, too-rye-a*
Today, today's a holiday
*John Kanaka-naka, too-rye-a*
Too-rye-a, ooh! too-tye-a
*John Kanaka-naka, too-rye-a*

We'll work tomorrow but not today
We'll work tomorrow but not today

We're bound away for Frisco Bay
We're bound away at the break of day

We're bound away around Cape Horn
Where you wish to God you'd never been born

Oh haul away, oh haul away
Oh haul away and earn your pay

A Liverpool ship and a Liverpool crew
And we're the boys to push her through

Just one more heave and that'll do
For we're the boys to pull her through

tan Hugill describes 'John Kanaka' as 'a very fine halyard shanty', learned from a Barbadian shantyman named 'Harding the Barbarian' with whom he sailed in the Pacific and around the West Indies between the wars. No earlier version of it than the one noted by him in 1961 seems to exist. 'Kanaka' refers to a native or inhabitant of Hawaii, while the original element of the refrain was 'tulai ē', derived from the Samoan language, so we're definitely in a Pacific state of mind here (despite the two 'Liverpool' verses included in this version). Hugill speculates that Western crews would have adapted aspects of the songs they heard being sung by Hawaiian men as they loaded ships in California in the 1830s.

Elsewhere, his description of the early nineteen-century despoliation of Hawaii by off-season American whalers makes for grim reading. In Australia, meanwhile, the term 'kanaka' described Pacific Islanders pressganged into agricultural work. Observations such as these remind us of the extent to which modern culture (including maritime culture, *including* the shanty) continues to bear the traces of the capitalist context within which it was produced.

The non-Western provenance of 'John Kanaka' may account for its somewhat unusual format, in which there are *three* (rather than the more ergonomic two or four) solo lines and refrains. 'The "oh" in the third solo', according to Hugill, 'was always rendered with a hitch (a sort of wild yelp)'; on the possibility, capability and advisability of attempting these 'original' shantyman stylings see 'A note on the material' (page 20).

I sing in a group which mashes 'John Kanaka' with the song 'We Will Rock You' by English rock band Queen. I have substituted the original 'tulai ē' element of the refrain with a more singable (and recognisably Irish) 'too-rye-a'.

A curious ritual associated with 'John Kanaka' exists in several versions on the Internet: a group of singers stands or sits by a long table, performing the shanty to a rhythm established by moving, tapping and throwing a number of cups or (less safely) glasses. The fact that there are versions of this routine from England, America and Germany points to the international scope of contemporary shanty culture.

*Then the Can, Boys, Bring, We'll Drink and Sing,*
illustration by V. Whall, 1910.

# 21. JOHNNY BOKER

Oh do me John-ny Bok-er, come rock and roll me o-o-ver, Do me John-ny Bo-ker, do!

Oh do me Johnny Boker, come rock and roll me over
*Do me Johnny Boker, do!*

Oh, do me Johnny Boker, we'll all go on a jamboree

Oh, do me Johnny Boker, the chief mate he's a croaker

Oh, do me Johnny Boker, the bosun's never sober

Oh, do me Johnny Boker, the skipper is a rover

Oh, do me Johnny Boker, the chips he ain't no sailor

Oh, do me Johnny Boker, the Packet is a-rolling

Oh, do me Johnny Boker, come roll me in the clover

Oh, do me Johnny Boker, we'll pull and haul together

Oh, do me Johnny Boker, me sweetheart's young and tender

Oh, do me Johnny Boker, we'll haul for better weather

Oh, do me Johnny Boker, from Calais down to Dover

Oh, do me Johnny Boker, and soon we'll be in London Town

Oh, do me Johnny Boker, one more pull then choke her

This was a popular 'sweating up' shanty used for various jobs requiring short pulls. The hauling action came on the last 'do' of the chorus, and was more of a communal grunt than a coherent articulation. Bert Lloyd provides a technical description of this kind of shanty:

*[The] solo line [is] usually in a metre of eight stresses, four plus four, and the refrain line basically a hexameter or octometer, but nearly always catalectic – that is, lacking a final beat – because of the combination of heavy emphasis and short syllable dictated by the sudden effort of hauling that occurs just as the sailors reach the end of their refrain.*

William Doerflinger traces this shanty's rather insalubrious North American provenance, writing that 'Johnny Boker': '…was one of the many characters shanghaied into shanty lore from the songs of the blackface minstrels, or possibly from Negro folksong, to which both sailors and minstrels were indebted.' In their *Ballads and Sea-Songs of Newfoundland* (1933), Elizabeth Greenleaf and Grace Mansfield make reference to a song entitled 'Jolly Poker', 'used to haul houses across the ice, boats on the land, and all kinds of heavy pulling'. The lines they cite – 'And it's O my jolly poker / And we'll start this heavy joker / And it's O my jolly poker-O' – clearly identify it as a version of the same song. Also, 'Boker' frequently became 'Booker', thereby providing plenty of 'humorous' rhyming opportunities for men at ease with 'industrial language'.

Of the numerous verses given here, probably only a few would have been required to complete the task in hand. In fact, 'Johnny Boker'[8] exists more as a virtual repository than an actual 'song', inasmuch as its melody was an empty vessel into which any of the standard shanty formulations could be poured, or material reused from other hauling shanties such as 'Haul on the Bowline' and 'Haul Away, Joe'.

Details from *The Difficult Passage,* anonymous print, c.1894.

# 22. LEAVE HER, JOHNNY, LEAVE HER

Oh the times are hard and the wages low
*Leave her, Johnny, leave her*
But now once more ashore we'll go
*It's time for us to leave her*
Leave her, Johnny, leave her
*Oh leave her, Johnny, leave her*
For the voyage is done and the winds don't blow
*It's time for us to leave her*

I thought I heard the captain say
Tomorrow we will get our pay

The work was hard and the voyage was long
The sea was high and the gales blew strong

Oh a dollar a day is a jackshite's pay
To pump all night and work all day

Heave one more turn and round she goes
Or each manjack will be kicking up his toes

Oh the rats have gone and as for the crew
It's time, me boys, that we went too

The winds were foul, the work was hard
From Liverpool Docks to Brooklyn Yard

We'll make her fast and stow our gear,
The gals are a-waiting on the pier

The winds were foul, the trip was long
But before we'll go we'll sing a song

A popular concept in contemporary cultural theory is the 'carnivalesque', by which is meant the temporary suspension of established authority – a time when, in the words of the great Jamaican cultural critic Stuart Hall, 'the people of "below" are granted the freedom both to revel in public and to comment on and satirise the actions and behaviour of those in authority'. Regarded by some as a vent for social pressures, carnivalesque seems to be a more or less universal phenomenon, observable in all parts of the world throughout history.

'Leave Her, Johnny, Leave Her' (also known as the 'Paying-off Shanty') might be considered in these terms because it was traditionally the last song sung before docking, and it afforded the sailors an opportunity to air their grievances against the people (owners, captain, officers, and so on) and the things (such as food and pay) that might have caused them grief during the voyage. As one may imagine, the most scurrilous material could be pressed into service time and again; and it must have been gratifying for the sailors to indulge opinions which at sea would have earned punitive action up to and including violence. Not much of that material has survived, either on account of its occasional nature or its censorship by the early collectors; even so, Stan Hugill is able to give 48 verses culled from various different capstan and pumping versions.

Surprise, engraving by Jacques La Grange, 1936.

# Sailortown

It has been suggested that the ocean and the port maintained a mutually dependent relationship during the great days of sail. The traversable *space* of the sea and the fixed *place* of the port – these were the co-ordinates which mapped the nautical imagination. Liverpool, London, Cardiff; Hamburg, Rotterdam, Marseilles; New York, Mobile, San Francisco; Singapore, Shanghai, Sydney: the great port cities of the world were always 'edgy' places – *literally*, in the sense that they developed on the geographical edge of the state-managed hinterland to which they ostensibly belonged; but also *symbolically* insofar as they were transnational, transitional spaces where the rule of law was tenuous and nothing was ever quite as it seemed.

All the great port cities developed their own 'Sailortown' – an area close to the docks ostensibly catering for the needs of the sailor. In fact, such areas tended to be concentrated centres of vice and violence. Stan Hugill wrote a book on the subject, describing Sailortown as:

…*a world of sordid pleasure, unlimited vice, and lashings of booze, but a dangerous place too … A sailor ashore was anything but safe. He was far safer at sea, hanging on by his eyebrows and toenails to an upper tops'l yard, reefing sail in a Cape Horn snifter, than he was in Sailortown, where every boarding-house master, harpy, pub hanger-on, and wharf-rat was waiting to skin or slug him, and where his useless corpse was often to be found, knife between the shoulder-blades, lying sprawled in some dark, dank alley, or coiled, obscenely, around a tide-washed, barnacled pile.*

Experienced sailors who 'knew the ropes' could generally negotiate the perils of Sailortown in safety. For younger men, even when pre-warned, it must have been difficult to resist the apparent 'pleasures' on offer – drinking, gambling, carousing and sex. It was only when these had metamorphosed into the horrors of kidnapping, theft, disease, assault and, not infrequently, death, that the darkness at the heart of Sailortown was revealed.

One of the principal occupations of the denizens of Sailortown was 'shanghaiing', also known as 'crimping'. The practice was elaborate and tended to be organised differently in different parts of the world, but in all places the aim was the same: to part the sailor from his pay and get him back to sea as quickly as possible. The deceptive woman is a recurring character here, captivating the sex-starved Sailor Jack so that her 'flashman' (pimp) can take advantage. We hear variations on this narrative in shanties such as 'Can't You Dance the Polka?' (No. 9) and 'Goodbye, Fare-Ye-Well' (No. 15), as well as in songs such as 'Go to Sea Once More' (No. 6) and 'Maggie May' (No. 9). Famous crimps included Liverpool's Paddy West, Larry Marr and Mike Connor of San Francisco, and Tommy Moore of Buenos Aires – Irishmen all, by the sound of their names. It was a profession, moreover, in which women could operate on equal terms, as the careers of San Francisco's Chloroform Kate and New York's Gallus Meg[9] attest.

Meg of Wapping, illustration by George Cruikshank, from Charles Dibden's Songs Naval and National, *1841*.

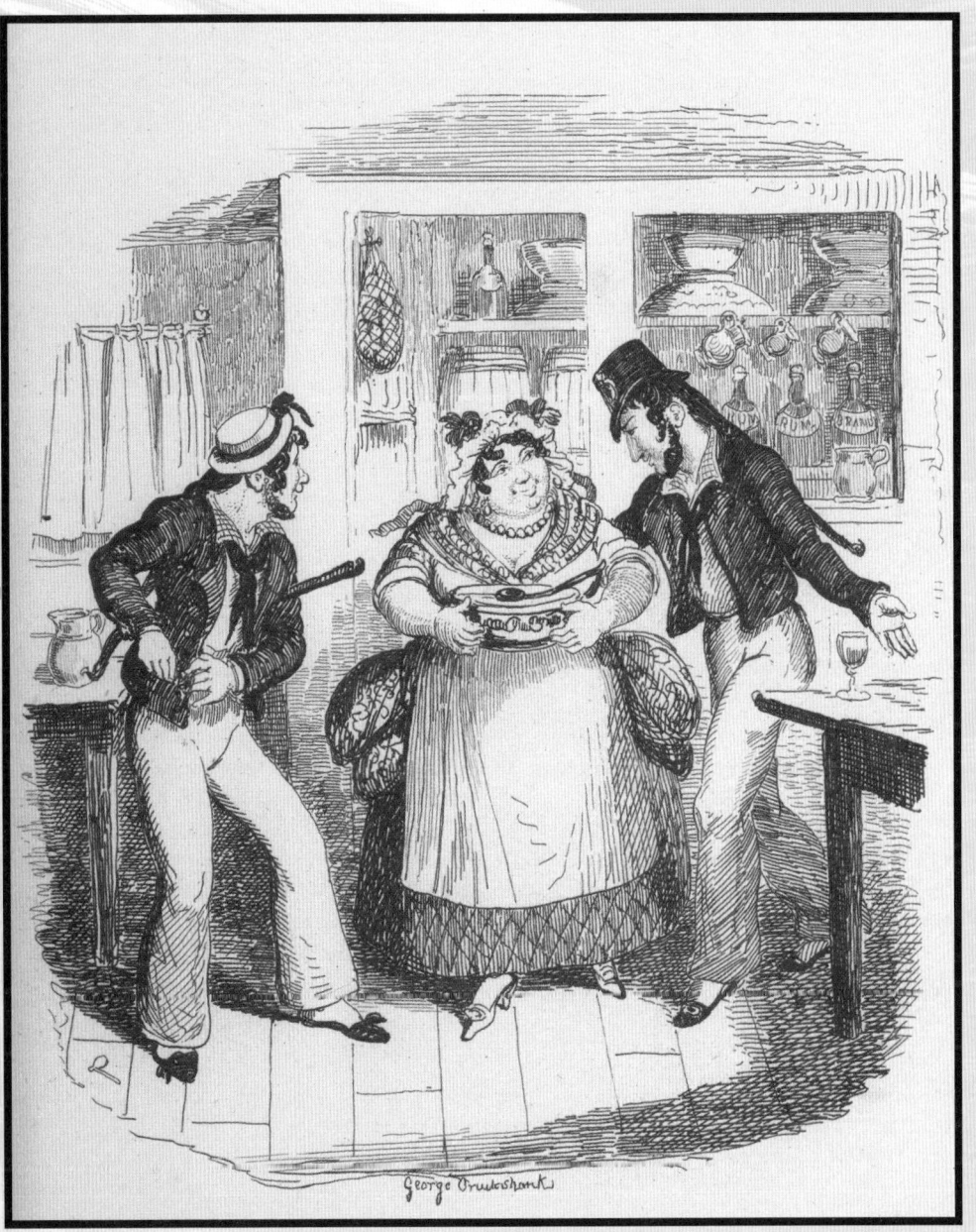

# 23. LIVERPOOL JUDIES

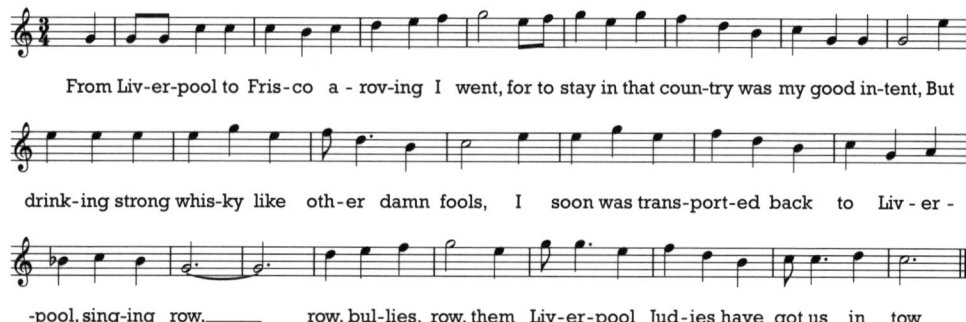

From Liv-er-pool to Fris-co a-rov-ing I went, for to stay in that coun-try was my good in-tent, But drink-ing strong whis-ky like oth-er damn fools, I soon was trans-port-ed back to Liv-er-pool, sing-ing row,___ row, bul-lies, row, them Liv-er-pool Jud-ies have got us in tow

From Liverpool to Frisco a-roving I went
For to stay in that country was my good intent
But drinking strong whisky like other damn fools
I soon was transported back to Liverpool ... singing
*Row, row, bullies, row*
*Them Liverpool Judies have got us in tow*

I shipped on the *Alaska* lying out in the bay
Waiting a fair wind to get under way
With all of her sailors so sick and so sore
They drunk all their whisky and can't get no more

Oh here comes the mate in a hell of a stew
He's looking for work for us sailors to do
Oh it's 'Fore tops'l halyards!' he loudly does roar
And it's 'Lay aloft Paddy, you son of a whore'

I remember the day we were crossing the line
When I think on it now, sure we had a good time
Diving bows under, the sailors all wet
She was doing twelve knots with the mainskys'l set

And now we've arrived in the Bramley-Moore Dock
And all the flash Judies on the Pierhead do flock
My money's all spent from my six quid advance
And I think it's high time, boys, to get up and dance

Here's a health to our captain wher'ere he may be
He's a friend to the sailor on land and on sea
But as for the chief mate, the dirty old brute
I hope when he dies straight to hell he'll skyhoot

The 'Row, Bullies, Row' refrain of this capstan shanty (which constitutes one of its alternative titles) may have been a mis-transcription by Cecil Sharp when he heard it sung in 1915 aboard the *St Paul* bound for New York: some authorities claim it should be 'roll, bullies, roll'. Certainly, 'rolling' (and its variants) tends to figure more strongly in the shanty lexicon than 'rowing', but it's Sharp's version that has prevailed. Hugill reckons this shanty originated with the Irish sailors who comprised the bulk of the Western Ocean packet crews after the 1840s. In his comments on 'Liverpool Judies' (which some singers change to 'Liverpool girls' because of the first term's residually offensive charge), he notes that it 'was usually sung in imitative Irish or Liverpool-Irish fashion'. Vocal imitation – in terms of accent, phrasing, vocabulary, and so forth – bespeaks (literally) a complex psychological response on the part of the imitator. What's going on when someone tries to imitate the voice, the accent, the mannerisms or the vocabulary of someone else? Leaving that aside, it's worthwhile acknowledging once again the extent of Irish influence on a range of popular musical styles and genres throughout the latter half of the nineteenth century.

Opened in 1848, Bramley-Moore Dock was designed by Jesse Hartley, who was the Superintendent of Liverpool's Dock Estate for nearly 40 years. 'Crossing the line' refers to the crossing of the equator during a voyage.

Ian Campbell sings a pretty racy 'crimping' version of 'Row, Bullies, Row' (featuring the great English fiddler Dave Swarbrick) on the album *Farewell Nancy* (1964).

# 24. LOWLANDS AWAY

I dreamed a dream the o-th-er-night, Low-lands,_ low-lands a-wa-y m-y

John,_ I dreamed a dream_ th-e o-th-er night, Low-la-nds aw-ay

I dreamed a dream the other night
*Lowlands, lowlands away my John*
I dreamed a dream the other night
*Lowlands away*

I dreamed I saw my own true love
He stood so still, he did not move

He came to me all dressed in white
All dressed in white like some fair bride

He made no sound, no words he said
And then I knew my love was dead

All dank his hair, all dim his eye
I knew that he had said goodbye

'I'm drowned in the Lowland Sea,' he said
'Oh, you and I will ne'er be wed'

I will cut away my bonnie hair
No other man will think me fair

My love is drowned in the windy Lowlands
My love is drowned in the windy Lowlands

Ah yes, but which 'lowlands' – Holland, Virginia, Scotland, Norfolk, the Caribbean? And about which scion of the extensive 'Lowlands' song family are we talking here? There was 'The Golden Vanity' variation sung to Stan Hugill by his father, about a cabin boy who rescues his ship from Spanish pirates only to be betrayed by his own captain – none other (according to Cecil Sharp, who included a version in his *A Book of British Song*) than that naughty Elizabethan rapscallion Sir Walter Raleigh. Then there was the version from the southern United States, forged by hoosiers in the melting pot of Mobile Bay and used, according to Captain Whall, at windlass and pumps. There was a West Indian version, used for halyard hauling, popular among the sugar and rum traders working out of Bristol. And then there's the mournful 'dream' variant – which is the one given here, poetically described by Laura Smith as 'the sighing of the wind and the throbbing of the restless ocean translated into melody'.

Although there exists a video of Stan Hugill singing this version of 'Lowlands Away' as a shanty, he was inclined to think it a shore-ballad with words uncharacteristically sentimental for working sailors. He repeats the point made by various other collectors, that its rhythmic irregularity (as well as its sentimentality) rendered it a less popular choice, although it was in fact used at different times for many shipboard chores.

'Lowlands Away' is unusual in that it deals with long – perhaps permanent – absence at sea from the perspective of those left behind. Among much that is ribald and facetious throughout the canon, such tragedy hits hard.

'Lowlands Away' is resistant to any strict time signature. Terry (3/4 and 2/4) and Sampson (3/2 and 2/2) try to circumvent this by introducing variant signatures. I've combined 4/4 with 3/4 here; but it's a compromise someway removed from the true spirit of the song, and Whall is probably closest to the mark when he writes that it should be sung 'quasi-recitative' – sung, that is, to the rhythms of ordinary speech.

The largest war ship, called den Eendracht, *Dutch print, 1704–1757.*

# 25. PADDY DOYLE'S BOOTS

Tim - me way - hey - ay - yah!    We'll pay Pad - dy Doyle for his boots

Timme way-hey-ay-yah!
We'll pay Paddy Doyle for his boots

Timme way-hey-ay-yah!
We'll all throw muck at the cook!

Timme way-hey-ay-yah!
We'll all drink brandy and gin!

Timme way-hey-ay-yah!
We'll all shave under the chin!

Technically, this is a different shanty from the others included in this volume, which as we've seen were typically of the 'heaving' and 'hauling' variety. 'Paddy Doyle's Boots' was one of a small number of 'bunting' or 'furling' shanties – as Bert Lloyd explains in his notes to the version he sings (along with Ewan MacColl) on the album *The Singing Sailor* (1954):

*Men aloft, furling the sail, would bunch the canvas till it formed a long bundle – the 'bunt'. To lift the bunt on to the yard, in order to lash it in position, required a strong heave. Bunt shanties differ from others in that they employed fewer voices, and were sung in chorus throughout.*

Stan Hugill disputes this last claim, and offers three different ways in which bunting shanties may have been used in practice. In any event, such songs were sung as sails were stowed on entering port, or when stormy weather demanded it. Bawdy verses (or lines) proliferated in this and in other occasional bunting shanties such as 'Johnny Boker', 'Boney Was a Warrior' and 'Haul Away, Joe'.

Who Paddy Doyle was and why his boots needed paying for remains unclear. James Healy claims that he was associated with Cobh, the port of Cork, on the southern coast of Ireland. But this particular 'Paddy' is often conflated with a different Irish boarding-house master and crimp – the notorious Paddy West, who operated out of Liverpool in the 1860s and 1870s, and who also had a well-known song named after him. One of Paddy West's income streams came from the fees generated by providing ships with 'experienced' crew members. In his backyard Paddy had a ship's wheel rigged up so the candidate could learn to steer, while his wife would chuck a bucket of cold water over the poor greenhorn to simulate life on the ocean wave. The young lad would practice furling sail on the curtains of the attic. Because that song is not included here, it's worth hearing, from Hugill, about another practice associated with both men:

*…the final ceremony was the stepping over a piece of string and the circling of a cow's horn standing on the front parlour table. 'When the mate axes ye where ye've sailed, tell him ye've crossed the Line, and bin three times around the Horn but don't tell him it wuz a cow's horn!' … [As] he trundled aboard with a sea-bag filled with bricks covered with an old jersey and a torn shirt, Farmer Jack, now Sailor John, had little idea of what awaited him out on the broad Atlantic!*

Funny, yes; but as so often with these songs and shanties, the actuality behind the humour bears consideration: the tender childhood, the young man, the call of the life adventurous, the initiation, and the first morning at sea when he wakes up to the reality of what he's let himself in for.

I'm Bound Away to
Leave You, *illustration*
*by V. Whall, 1910.*

# 26. PADDY, LAY BACK

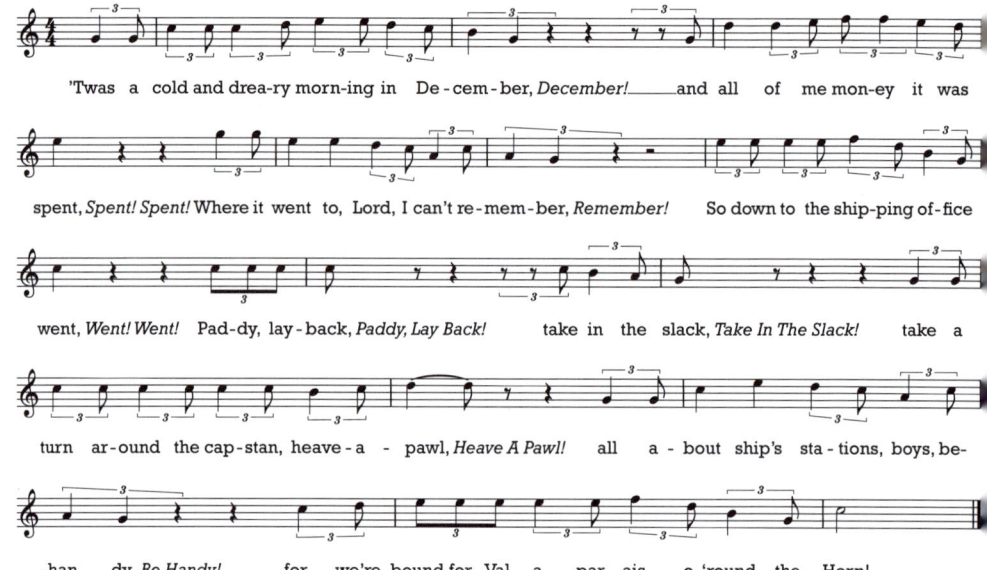

'Twas a cold and dreary morning in December, *December!*
And all of me money it was spent, *Spent! Spent!*
Where it went to, Lord, I can't remember, *Remember!*
So down to the shipping office went, *Went! Went!*

CHORUS:
Paddy, lay back, *Paddy, Lay Back!*
Take in the slack, *Take In The Slack!*
Take a turn around the capstan, heave a pawl, *Heave A Pawl!*
All about ship's stations, boys, be handy, *Be Handy!*
For we're bound for Valaparaiso 'round the Horn!

That day there was a great demand for sailors
For the colonies, for Frisco and for France
So I signed aboard a Limey barque, the *Hotspur*
Got paralytic drunk on my advance

I woke up in the morning sick and sore
And knew I was outward bound again
When I heard a voice a-bawling at the door
'Lay aft, men, and answer to your names!'

'Twas on the quarterdeck where first I saw them
Such an ugly bunch I'd never seen afore
For there was a bum and stiff from every quarter
And it made me poor old heart feel sick and sore

Although my poor old head was all a-jumping
We had to loose her rags the following morn
I dreamt the boarding-master I was thumping
When I found out he'd sent me around the Horn

I quickly made my mind up I would jump her
I'd leave the beggar and get a job ashore
I swum across the Bay and went and left her
And in the English Bar I found a whore

But Jimmy the Crimp he knew a thing or two, sir
And soon he'd shipped me outward bound
    again
On a Limey to the Chinchas for guano, boys
And soon I was a-roaring this refrain

So there was I once more again at sea, boys
The same old ruddy business over again
Oh, stamp the capstan round and make some
    noise, boys
And sing again this dear old sweet refrain

Here we have a celebrated example – along with 'Paddy West', 'Paddy Doyle's Boots' and 'Paddy Works on the Railway' – of a genre of work songs celebrating the nickname once used ubiquitously for the sons of Erin wherever (and doing whatever) they might happen to fetch up.

Also known as 'Valparaiso 'Round the Horn' and 'Mainsail Haul', this multi-verse forebitter and shanty tells the classic tale of a ragbag crew and a feckless sailor cheated and mistreated at every turn. Its solo/refrain disposition is unusual, as is its deployment of technical language: a 'pawl', Douglas Morgan tells us, 'is part of a ratchet device which allows the capstan to turn in only one direction'.

The song was popular with different maritime professions at various times throughout the nineteenth century, including the guano trade (mentioned in the penultimate verse) in which vast amounts of seabird excrement were shipped to Europe and North America where it was used for fertiliser and in the production of explosives.

## 27. REUBEN RANZO

Oh poor old Reu-ben Ran-zo, Ran-zo, boys, Ran-zo, Oh pi-ty poor Reu-ben Ran-zo, Ran-zo, boys, Ran-zo

Oh poor old Reuben Ranzo
*Ranzo, boys, Ranzo*
Oh pity poor Reuben Ranzo
*Ranzo, boys, Ranzo*

Oh, Ranzo was no sailor
So he shipped on board a whaler

Ranzo was no beauty
So he could not do his duty

They put him holystoning
And cared not for his groaning

Because he was so dirty
They gave him five-and-thirty

The skipper's daughter Suzie
Well she begged her dad for mercy

She gave him wine and water
And a bit more than she ought to

She gave him rum and whisky
Which made him feel so frisky

She taught him navigation
And a whaler's education

Well he got his first mate papers
He's a terror to the whalers

Now he's known wherever them whale fish blow
As the hardest bastard on the go

his was a favourite hauling song in British and American ships, and was also one of a few shanties to be employed on whalers. Captain Whall claimed there was a master version that suffered no deviation, although in fact numerous versions (including some Scandinavian ones) are extant.

The identity of the eponymous sailor has been the subject of much speculation – by turns he was a Portuguese whaler, a sixteenth-century Danish patriot, a Russian (or Polish) Jewish tailor, or an American novice. Stan Hugill makes a good case for Ranzo as a Sicilian emigrant tormented for his 'dirty' Italian habits.

Regarding hygiene at sea, the 'holystoning' mentioned in the fourth verse refers to one of the least popular shipboard tasks: the scouring of the wooden deck with a piece of soft sandstone. Despite this and other efforts to remain 'shipshape', the life nautical was not generally conducive to good health. Disease was common (even after the discovery in the eighteenth century of citrus fruit as a means to resist scurvy). The exertions of deep-sea labour took a heavy toll.

Ranzo's fate is equally uncertain: in the version included here (derived in the main from Bert Lloyd's 1957 recording) he marries the captain's daughter and ascends to his own command, whereas in others he is tossed overboard for being so dirty or simply lashed ('five-and-thirty') for stealing.

Richard Terry used 'Reuben Ranzo' to demonstrate the 'long hoist' hauling technique, with the pulls coming on the two *Ran* stresses in the response. He also supplied three different melodic variations. Although the melody supplied by Laura Smith back in 1888 was slightly different to the one used here (the one most frequently sung today), she found it 'mournful and almost haunting in its monotony' – a fitting testament for Reuben's elusive career.

A Narwhal, *illustration from* The Strand Magazine, *January 1897.*

# 28. RIO GRANDE

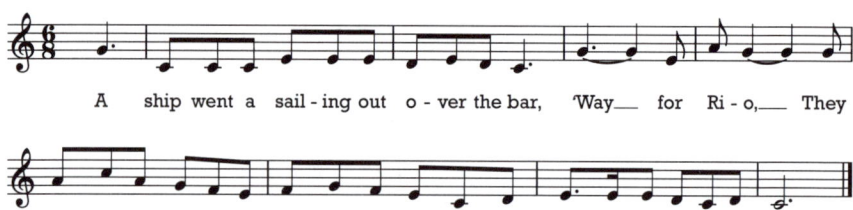

A ship went a sail-ing out o-ver the bar, 'Way for Ri-o, They point-ed her bow to the Sou-the-rn Star, and we're bound for the R-i-o Grande

A ship went a sailing out over the bar
'Way for Rio
They pointed her bow to the Southern Star
And we're bound for the Rio Grande

CHORUS:
And it's away, bullies, away, away for Rio
We're singing farewell to them Liverpool girls
And we're bound for the Rio Grande

Oh say were you never down Rio Grande?
Them smart senoritas they sure beat the band

We were sick of the beach when our money was gone
So we signed on this packet to drive her along

There's some of us sick, aye, and some of us sore
We've scoffed all our whack and we're looking for more

Our anchor we'll weigh and the rags we will set
Them Liverpool Judies we'll never forget

You Parkee Lane Judies we'll have you to know,
We're bound to the south'ard, oh Lord let us go

O pack up your donkeys and get under way,
Them Judies we're leaving will get our half-pay

Cheer up, Mary Ellen, and don't look so glum,
On white-stocking day you'll be drinking hot rum.

It's goodbye to Ellen and sweet Molly too
And the Judies of Bootle, 'tis goodbye to you

Saltfish and lobscouse for the next half a year
She's a Liverpool packet and her Old Man's the gear

*The four-masted barque* Olivebank *in the North Atlantic. Between 1882 and 1922.*

**D**escribed by Stan Hugill as 'probably the most popular "outward-bounder" of them all', this capstan shanty exists in many versions and has been performed and recorded widely since it was first collected. Stuart Frank writes that the melody of 'Rio Grande' (invariably pronounced 'Rye-o') 'was evidently imported virtually unchanged from Cameroon', and points out that the place-name refers not 'to the river forming the Mexico–Texas border, but to the Rio Grande de la Plata in South America'. Hugill, as is his wont, favours a Liverpool setting: 'white-stocking day' refers to the practice (extant to the middle decades of the twentieth century) whereby Mrs Sailor would don her best clothes when collecting her husband's half-pay at the local shipping office.

Laura Smith records two versions, including one involving a 'pretty young maid' (which scans the same as 'Liverpool girl') clearly adapted from the folk song 'Where are you going, my pretty fair maid?' She found the melody 'very mournful', despite its bouncy rhythm. Captain Whall cites an American version (involving 'Thanksgiving Day' rather than 'white-stocking day'), while Richard Terry's version manages to slip in lyrics from a wide array of sources: 'I used to notice, even as a boy', he writes, 'how [this beautiful shanty] used to inspire the shantyman to sentimental flights of *Heimweh* [homesickness] that at times came perilously near poetry.' This assessment is supported by Bert Lloyd, who notes that a version of this shanty was collected in 1908 from the Dartmouth shantyman John Perring by the composer Percy Grainger, who considered his source to be 'one of the most creatively gifted, fiery-spirited traditional singers' he had ever heard, a man who invested shanties 'with a strange blend of sea-born weirdness and human tenderness'.

I think it's this combination of weirdness and tenderness that continues to draw people to what is a residual tradition, and which ensures that so long as we continue to find meaning and value in singing, so long will the shanties themselves survive.

# Bawdy

'Bawdy' refers to lyrical material regarded as risqué by the politer echelons of society – what Stan Hugill once referred to as 'non-drawing-room verses'. Sailors would have been prohibited from singing indecent material within hearing of ticketed passengers; in other contexts, however, they did what sequestered groups of ordinary men have probably always done and sang about sex in the most graphic and most 'comedic' of terms they could invent: prostitution, female anatomy, sexually transmitted disease, homosexuality, bestiality, and the fullest range of sexual techniques and predilections imaginable – 'the veriest filth' according to W.B. Whall – and all wind to the shantyman's sails.

The American scholar Gershon Legman devoted his career to the study of erotica and sexual humour – in particular, the folk lore and psychological signature of the dirty joke. In *The Horn Book: Studies in Erotic Folklore and Bibliography* (1963), he turned his attention to the bawdy ballad and the 'chanty', suggesting that:

*[exposed] to danger at all times by reason of their trade, the sailors sang songs that have always been notably obscene ... [The] riotous obscenity of these songs ... gives expression to the anger – in psycho-analytical terms the 'anal sadism' – of these men, deprived of all possibility of natural sex lives for long periods, during the fullest years of their virile strength.*

Prisoners, soldiers, sailors, lumberjacks, students, sports teams – the folk canon is replete with the songs that these groups of men sang about what wasn't currently available.

Whatever its root cause, there can be no doubting either the deeply salacious nature of much shanty material, nor the dilemma facing the first non-participant respondents to the genre. Colourful characters coping with difficult circumstances was one thing; obscenity and indecency (as defined by late-Victorian scholars and early twentieth-century publishers) was something else again. Legman pointed out that the shanties had only ever 'appeared in pitifully expurgated form', and deplored '[the] falsified record of synthetic folksong which is neither scholarly enough for real scholars, nor "popular" enough to be accepted by the folk'. It's certainly the case that generations of collector-critics have avoided committing sexually explicit lyrics to paper. Scholarly propriety thus played as important a role in the emergence of a shanty canon as it did in the formation of other elements of the 'folk revival'. Even the former shantyman Stan Hugill (with whom Legman corresponded) danced a

hornpipe around the issue, consistently reworking what he referred to as the 'original Liverpool versions' in order to avoid words and images that might offend his readers.

The issue of scholarly bowdlerisation has not gone away; indeed, in the 'woke' culture of the early twenty-first century, the issue of how to engage with sensitive material (including bawdy) has become even more fraught (see the commentary on 'The Hog-Eye Man', No. 19). Most commentators locate themselves somewhere along a continuum running between completely accurate reproduction (so far as it's available) and politically sensitive 'reconstructions', considered in the light of current concerns. The lyrics included in this volume tend towards the latter end of this scale, although it is possible to locate versions closer to the originals.

Saturday Night at Sea, *illustration by George Cruikshank, from Charles Dibden's* Songs Naval and National, *1841.*

# 29. ROLL, ALABAMA, ROLL

Oh in eigh-teen hun-dred and six-ty-one, Roll, Al-a-ba-ma, roll,

This ship build-ing was be-gun, Oh roll, Al-a-ba-ma, roll!

Oh in eighteen hundred and sixty-one
*Roll, Alabama, roll!*
This shipbuilding was begun
*Oh, roll, Alabama, roll!*

When the *Alabama*'s keel was laid
It was laid in the yard of Jonathan Laird

It was laid in the yard of Jonathan Laird
It was laid in the town of Birkenhead

At first she was called the Two-Nine-O
For the merchants of the city of Liverpool

Down the Mersey river she sailed then
Livorpool fitted her with guns and men

From the Western Isles she sailed forth
To destroy the commerce of the north

She sailed the sea for two whole years
Took sixty-five ships in her career

To Cherbourg port she went one day
For to take her count of prize money

Many a sailor he saw his doom
When the *Kearsarge* hoved into view

'Twas a ball from the forward pivot that day
Blew the *Alabama*'s stern away

On June nineteen 1864
The *Alabama* went to the cold ocean floor

*Captain Raphael Semmes, Alabama's commander (foreground), with First Lieutenant John M. Kell (background).*

**T**he *Alabama* was a Confederate ship built to harass Union commerce during the American Civil War. The song tells the story more or less accurately – how the '290' was commissioned and constructed in secret at John Laird, Sons and Company shipyard in Birkenhead on the banks of the Mersey – later, the world-famous Cammell Laird shipbuilding company; how it was funded in part by speculative capital operating out of Liverpool; how it was launched as the *Enrica* on 15 May 1862, before being refitted as the CSS *Alabama* once out of (neutral) British waters; how it was manned by a partially English crew attracted by the promise of war plunder; how it wreaked havoc on Yankee shipping all around the world (including the Atlantic, Indian and Pacific Oceans) during the course of a two-year career; how it was sunk near Cherbourg Harbour on 19 June 1864 by the USS *Kearsarge* – a sloop-of-war (named after Mount Kearsarge in the state of New Hampshire) launched in 1861 specifically to combat Confederate commerce raiders.

This version misses out the part in which 41 of the *Alabama*'s crew, including Captain Raphael Semmes, escaped on a yacht named the *Deerhound* owned by the British Liberal politician John Lanchester – so much for neutrality.

Only Stan Hugill and William Doerflinger have 'Roll, *Alabama*, Roll' as a shanty – the first at halyards, the second at pumps. Hugill also makes the point that 'roll' vies with 'blow' and 'hilo' as the most popular word in the sailor's lexicon.

# 30. SALLY BROWN

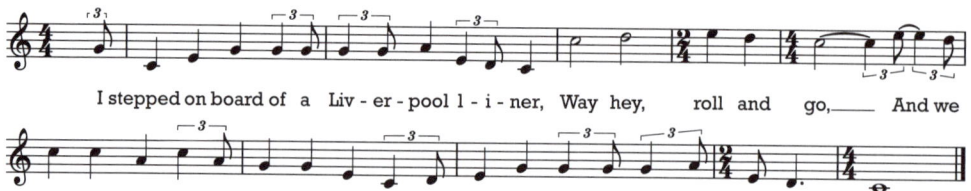

I stepped on board of a Liverpool liner
   *Way-hey, roll and go*
And we rolled all night and we rolled all day
   *Gonna spend my money 'long with Sally Brown*

Sally lives in old Jamaica
Selling rum and growing tobacco

Sally lives on the old plantation
She is a daughter of the Wild Goose Nation

Seven long years I courted Sally
But all she did was dilly-dally

Sally Brown, what is the matter?
Pretty girl but can't get at her

Her mother doesn't like no tarry sailor
So I shipped away in a New Bedford whaler

Sally Brown I long to see you
Sally Brown, I'll not deceive you

Captain Frederick Marryat, an important contributor to the literary genre of the sea adventure, reported hearing a version of this capstan shanty while sailing to the United States in the 1830s. One hopes that any gentle souls aboard were spared the more salacious descriptions of the adventures of Sally and her mother.

I came across 'Sally Brown' as a song included on an album by the 1960s folk group Sweeney's Men, where it was sung by two stalwarts of the Irish folk scene: Andy Irvine (who went on to play with Planxty) and Terry Woods (a member of the classic Pogues line-up). Their version seems to me to have a kind of reggae pulse running throughout, with emphases (unusual for most Western and popular musical forms) on the second and fourth beats of the four-beat bar. I was intrigued subsequently to discover that the song's origins are probably West Indian – Jamaican, in fact, where (according to collectors such as Anne Gilchrist and Stan Hugill) it was still being used as a log-rolling work song as late as the 1930s.

We know that reggae didn't appear in Jamaica until the late-1960s, as an offshoot of the styles known as 'ska' and 'rocksteady'. There's nothing in the lyrics of the Sweeney's Men version to suggest a Jamaican origin; besides, I find it impossible to credit that Irvine and Woods – musically adventurous though they were – would have known of this new genre, or would have attempted to reproduce it even if they had. Rather, I incline to the belief that 'Sally Brown' already contained the rhythmic characteristics – that skank riddim on the off-beat, derived no doubt from Africa originally and transported to the West Indies along with the slaves – that eventually makes its way into reggae via ska and rocksteady.

There has been much thought given to the derivation and meaning of the phrase 'Wild Goose Nation' (which also crops up in a shanty not included in this volume, 'We'll Ranzo Way' also known as 'The Wild Goose Shanty'). The 'Wild Geese' of history were those Jacobites who chose permanent exile from their Irish homeland after defeat in the Williamite Wars of the late-seventeenth century. In those terms it might have been adopted by others – transported slaves, for example – who underwent a similar experience of enforced removal from their ancestral homeland. But that is, and must remain, conjecture.

'There's a Whale-Fish' He Cried, *illustration by V. Whall, 1910.*

# 31. SANTIANA

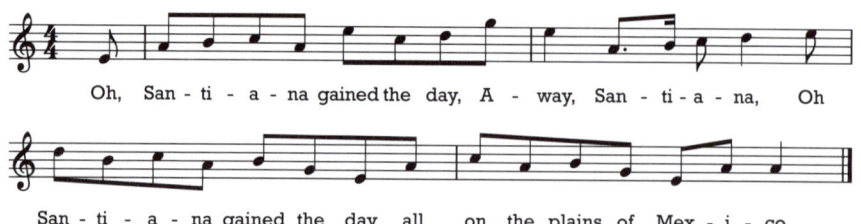

Oh, Santiana gained the day
*Away, Santiana*
Oh, Santiana gained the day
*All on the plains of Mexico*

Oh Mexico, oh Mexico,
Oh Mexico where I must go

He gained the day at Molly-del-rey
And General Taylor ran away

Oh Santiana fought for fame
And Santiana gained a name

Santiana's men were true and brave
Many found a hero's grave

Santiana was a damn fine man
Till he ran afoul of Uncle Sam

Oh Santiana's day is o'er
Santiana will fight no more

Now Santiana shovels gold
Around Cape Horn in the ice and cold

We'll dig his grave with a silver spade
And mark the spot where he was laid

**A**lso known as 'Santy Anna' and 'The Plains of Mexico', this shanty exists in a number of variants which were intermingled in practice. One strand extols the delights of exotic female company in a manner unlikely to find favour today. Another focused (highly inaccurately, as it happens) on the nineteenth-century Mexican soldier and politician Antonio de Padua María Severino López de Santa Aña y Pérez de Lebrón (1795–1876) – only part of whose name, thankfully, features in the shanty itself! Along with the likes of Simon Bolivar and Bernardo O'Higgins, Santa Aña was one of the heroic figures from South America's revolutionary century. Even so, he couldn't halt the United States's annexation of large swathes of the Mexican Empire, including the resource-rich territories of Texas, New Mexico and California.

Santa Aña did not 'gain the day'; he was in fact narrowly defeated by General (later President) Zachary Taylor at the Battle of Buena Vista (Molina del Rey – the 'Molly-del-rey' of verse three) in 1847, nine years after the Alamo and the rather less-well-known Goliad Massacre in which upwards of 400 Texan prisoners of war were executed, apparently under direct orders from the *Generalissimo* himself.

Stan Hugill notes a possibility that this song refers to Anne, patron saint of Breton sailors. He also alludes to a much older (sixteenth-century) Mediterranean pirate-hunting vessel named *Santa Anna*. Most authorities (including W. B. Whall, Richard Terry and Bert Lloyd) lean towards the Mexican connection, however. Laura Smith cites 'Santy Anna' as a windlass shanty adapted from early nineteenth-century slaves, for whom their enemy's enemy (which is to say, the American state) would have been a friend. The shanty was popular with British sailors, who (for both political and commercial reasons) likewise harboured a residual resentment towards their American cousins, as well as a fondness for Gulf ports such as Altamira and Veracruz.

'Santiana' displays melodic links with other minor key shanties such as 'Whip Jamboree' and 'Clear the Track, Let the Bullgine Run'. Although 'grand chorus' versions exist (which is to say, a four-line refrain sung by all), the version given here has a clear two-line solo/refrain structure, rendering it a typical heaving shanty for use at pumps or windlass.

With Her Pistols Loaded
She Went Aboard,
*illustration by V. Whall, 1910.*

# 32. SHALLOW BROWN

Oh I'm bound a-way to leave you, Shal-low,— oh Shal-low Brown, Oh I

nev-er will de-ceive you,— Shal-low,— oh Shal-low Brown

Oh I'm bound away to leave you
*Shallow, oh Shallow Brown*
Oh I never will deceive you
*Shallow, oh Shallow Brown*

Oh the packet leaves tomorrow
This parting brings me sorrow

In the cradle is my baby
I want no other lady

My clothes are all in pawn
I'm bound around the Horn

I'll cross the Chile mountains
To pump the silver fountains

Be on the pier to meet me
With kisses I will greet you

She won't miss me when I've gone
She'll hook some other bum

This shanty is also known as 'Challo Brown' – 'challo' being a word used in the Caribbean to describe someone with ancestry predating the European influx. Many commentators regard this halyard shanty – described as 'beautiful' by Richard Terry – as a hybrid of ship song and slave song: the former (about the sailor's separation from his native love) latching opportunistically onto the latter – about the tragedy of enforced separation.

Another issue of interest lies in the fact that 'Shallow Brown' was one of the first shanties to make its way into the art tradition. In 1901 the young Australian composer Percy Grainger moved to London where he came under the influence (paradoxically middle-class and metropolitan) of the burgeoning folk movement. Besides being an assiduous collector he was also interested in the aesthetic qualities of folk song. In 1908 he transcribed 'Shallow Brown' after listening to the singing of a man named John Perring from the seaside town of Dartmouth in Devon. A few years later Grainger set the song for orchestra, voice and chorus with the intention, as he wrote, of suggesting the 'wafted, wind-borne, surging sounds heard at sea'.

The question of his success (or otherwise) in this endeavour broaches a series of issues which go straight to the heart of the entire British folk movement of the last 150 years. Some people will hear Grainger's setting and give themselves up to the dignity and the elemental pathos of the emotion; others will hear only exploitation and misunderstanding – yet another instance of the empowered intellectual descending from 'the light' to gaze condescendingly upon the denizens of the dark. Where we position ourselves in terms of this debate has major implications for the way we understand the world and ourselves in relation to it. Who knew shanties were so important?

## 33. SHENANDOAH

Oh Shen-an-doah,___ I long to hear you,___ A - way,___ you roll-ing riv-er,___ 'Cross that wide___ and roll-ing riv-er,___ A - way, I'm bound a-way 'cross the wide Mis-sour-i___

Oh Shenandoah, I long to hear you
   *Away, you rolling river*
'Cross that wide and rolling river
   *Away, I'm bound away 'cross the wide*
   *Missouri*

Oh Missouri she's a mighty river
The Indian camp lies on the border

The white man loved the Indian maiden
With notions his canoe was laden

'Oh, Shenandoah, I love your daughter
I'll take her 'cross yon rolling water'

The chief disdained the trader's dollars
'My daughter never you shall follow'

At last there came a Yankee skipper
He winked his eye and tipped his flipper

He sold the chief that fire-water
And 'cross the river stole his daughter

aura Smith appears to get this famous shanty (which she calls 'Shenandore') mixed up with 'Sally Brown' and 'Rio Grande' – one wonders if she wasn't on occasion the target of some tarry humour as she wandered the county (Northumberland) looking for material. On the other hand, Stan Hugill notes that the name 'Shenandoah' was frequently substituted by one of the figures from the shanty pantheon – 'Sally Brown' 'Paddy Doyle', and so on, and because there was a great deal of swapping of lyrics and melodic features between songs, Smith (and her source) may be forgiven on this occasion.

Clearly North American in derivation, this shanty started life as a folk song about an encounter between white settlers and Native Americans. The story of a white man's love for a native woman echoes the famous, supposed liaison between Captain John Smith and Pocahontas.

Shenandoah (Skenandoa) was an important figure in eighteenth-century American history: elected chief of the Onieda tribe, British ally in the Seven Years' War, patriot ally in the American Revolutionary War and centurion (1710–1816, he died aged 105). There are different accounts of the song's emergence – riverine, portside, mountainy, military. Once established, however, it was adapted for different ends: besides the nativist context featured here, there were popular slave and geo-colonial versions. In relation to the latter, the state of Virginia got itself in an embarrassing pickle in 2006 by confusing these versions when it was looking for a state song.

'Shenandoah' was a typical capstan and windlass shanty, its slow tempo and numerous verse-chorus repetitions being conducive to the particularly onerous task of anchor-raising. The song's sentimental melody line also made it highly amenable to harmonisation; even if the sailors themselves didn't attempt it, this feature has been widely exploited in the song's post-shanty career – notably Percy Grainer's cloyingly lush setting. The list of people who have recorded versions reads like a *Who's Who* of modern popular music – everyone from Paul Robeson to Judy Garland and Bruce Springsteen to Hayley Westenra.

Shenandoah: The White Man Loved the Indian Maiden, *illustration by V. Whall, 1910.*

# 34. SO HANDY, MY GIRLS

So han-dy, me boys, so han-dy, so han-dy, me girls, so han-dy, Why

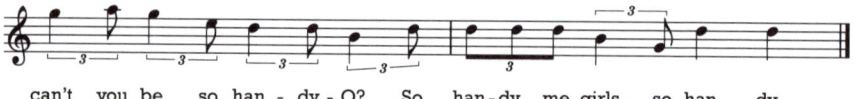
can't you be so han-dy-O? So han-dy, me girls, so han-dy

So handy, me boys, so handy
*So handy, me girls, so handy*
Why can't you be so handy-O?
*So handy, me girls, so handy*

Oh stretch it aft and start a song
A damn fine song and it won't take long

Be handy in the morning
Be handy in the morning

Oh we are outward bound, you know
Oh we are outward bound you know

Oh, up aloft that yard must go,
Oh, up aloft from down below.

Growl ye may but go ye must
It matters not whether last or first

Oh, a bully ship and a bully crew
We're the gang for to kick her through

Your advance has gone, you're at sea again
Bound round the Horn through the hail and rain

Oh up aloft with tautened leach
Hand-over-hand gang ye must reach

Round Cape Horn we're bound to go
Round Cape Stiff through the ice and snow

Sing and haul, and haul and sing
Up aloft this yard we'll swing

Up aloft that yard must go
For we are outward bound, you know

Be handy with your washing, girls,
O can't you be so handy-O

My love she is a dandy-O
And she is fond of brandy-O

A handy ship and a handy crew
A handy mate and Old Man too

I thought I heard the Old Man say
Another pull and then belay

Although this song was collected by Cecil Sharp in 1914 from one of the fountainheads of the modern shanty canon, 'Yankee Jack' Short, many other sources prefer a male presence ('my boys') in the refrain. Captain Whall goes for 'girls' in his truncated version (only two verses), and Richard Terry has 'gels'. John Sampson's version favours 'boys' over 'girls', and is just a catalogue of maritime professions, including 'bose' (boatswain), 'sails' (sailmaker) and 'chips' (carpenter).

Most versions of this well-known and widely used halyard shanty are comprised of stock lines interspersed with the same 'Handy' refrain. Joanna Colcord wrote that it was a sort of 'general utility' shanty with no fixed words and no fixed story lines. Stan Hugill's 'boys' version has 24 verses, many of which were deployed liberally throughout the shanty canon: the ship is always bully, the advance is always spent, here we go again around Cape Stiff in the ice and snow, and so on. The one version that seems to buck the trend is Laura Smith's early ('boys') version, which tells a coherent folk tale about Jack's courtship and desertion of a serving girl named Sarah Jane.

One of the shanty's defining characteristics is, as pointed out in the introduction, the use of a repertoire of stock phrases. In light of that, it's worth considering that

the ancient Greek word *rhapsōidia*, from which we get rhapsody, means 'to stitch together', and the shantyman functioned (like versifying storytellers throughout history) as an assembly-line worker *stitching together* a series of prefabricated elements – 'set expressions', as Walter Ong writes, which they 'preserved and/or reworked largely for metrical purposes'. The aesthetic values of the shanty may jar with those of a highly literate culture such as ours, but that doesn't make them any less beautiful or any less powerful.

Heaving the Lead, illustration from J.A. Atkinson, A Picturesque Representation of the Naval, Military and Miscellaneous Costumes of Great Britain, *1807.*

# 35. SOUTH AUSTRALIA

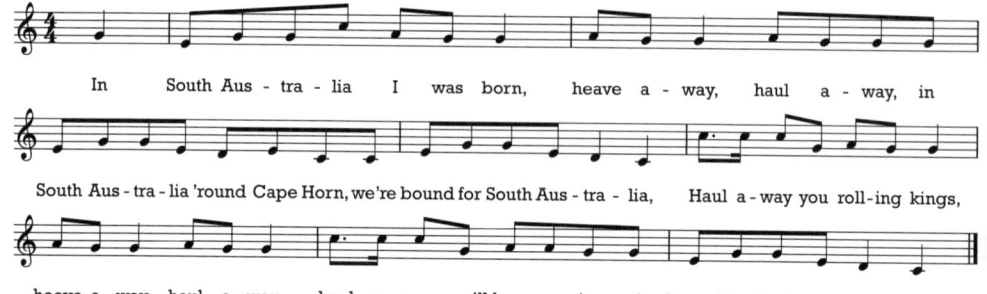

In South Australia I was born
*Heave away, haul away*
In South Australia 'round Cape Horn
*We're bound for South Australia*
Haul away you rolling kings
*Heave away, haul away*
Haul away, you'll hear me sing
*We're bound for South Australia*

As I walked out one morning fair
'Twas there I met Miss Nancy Blair

I shook her up, I shook her down
I shook her round and round the town

I run her all night and I run her all day
I run her 'til we sailed away

There ain't but one thing grieves my mind
To leave Miss Nancy Blair behind

And as we wallop round Cape Horn
You'll wish to God you'd never been born

The Packet Ship, illustration by Gordon Grant from Henry B. Culver, The Book of Old Ships, *1924*.

Australia first impinged on the Eurocentric imagination after it was 'discovered' by Captain James Cook in 1770. The continent doesn't feature particularly strongly in the shanty canon, which was dominated in the main by the Atlantic theatre of operations. This is interesting in itself, given the volume of trade (goods such as wool and wheat) and human traffic with Australia during the shanty's nineteenth-century heyday. Despite the cessation in 1868 of criminal transportation to the Antipodes, the prospect of 'Botany Bay' and 'Van Diemen's Land' lived long in the folk memory of the British Isles.

Laura Smith gives a long version of 'South Australia', collected from a Newcastle seaman, in *Music of the Waters*; this version references a 'ruler king' (as opposed to 'rolling king') and had a double 'heave away' chorus where the subsequently popular 'heave away, haul away' refrain was. Thereafter 'South Australia' seems to have developed a predominantly American flavour, with two main variants – one involving a 'good' sailor returning to his wife, the other a more liberated chap discoursing on the pleasures of the girls of Cape Cod (or Liverpool or London or Cardiff, if the ship was British).

The most popular current version (the one taught by the Irish singer-songwriter Terry Woods to the rest of the Pogues for the version included on the band's 1987 album *If I Should Fall From Grace With God*) is the one recorded by Irish-American ballad group the Clancy Brothers in 1962, which they describe as 'a lively, optimistic sailors' song'. In the process they changed Bert Lloyd's 'lollop' – as in 'lollop around Cape Horn' – to the much more descriptive Irishism, 'wallop'.

In some ways, 'South Australia' encapsulates – paradoxically, as it happens – the essence of shanty discourse insofar as it was sung at capstan *and* pumps; it functioned as both a shanty *and* a forebitter; it was adapted and sung in both the Atlantic *and* the Pacific; there are versions featuring 'good' *and* 'bad' sailors; and so on. Like life itself, the shanty is *both/and*, rather than *either/or*. This binary ambivalence extends to the physical movement described in the song's refrain (and alternative title): heave away, haul away. Stan Hugill (whose version at the Workum International Shanty Festival in 1990 is available to view on the Internet) tells us that: '[normally] the words "heave" and "haul" are not mixed in shanties, the former being found only in capstan songs, the latter in halyard shanties.' Here, however, they are not out of place, as some men 'would be "heaving away" at the pump handles and others "hauling away" at the "bell ropes"'.

# Folk or Fake?

In his book *One For the Money: Politics and Popular Song* (1980), Dave Harker's[10] view of the English folk revival is clear and stark:

*What Sharp and his coadjutors did was impose on to the living culture of English working people ... in some parts of some predominantly rural counties in the south-west, notions of history and of culture which owe more to romance than to reality.*

For Harker, the English folk revival served as a clear example of what the late historian Eric Hobsbawm described as 'the invention of tradition'. This refers to the process whereby ideas of 'normality', supposedly inherited from the past, are established in the present through ritual and constant repetition – the idea that if enough people say or do the same thing often enough it will come to seem natural and true. Such ideas, moreover, are always morally and politically inflected: it's *right and good* to be in touch with the past; it's *right and good* to honour our ancestors and to keep the old ways alive; it's *right and good* to celebrate and practice what 'we' have always done, and always done differently from others.

Tradition is especially important during times of rapid change, as communities find their established values coming under pressure from a variety of sources. That's exactly the situation we find in Britain during the late-nineteenth and early twentieth centuries: suddenly the world is much older than we thought (Darwin); God is dead (Nietzsche) and time is relative (Einstein); class struggle is paramount (Marx) and sex is paramount (Freud); identity (racial, gender, sexual) is the watchword. The present is a much different

country to the one in which our parents and grandparents grew up. In such a context, it's no wonder that people want to cling to the certainties of the past; and it's no wonder, if those certainties aren't clear or are simply unavailable, that they should be invented.

Understood in such terms, the folk revival's implicit task was to 'identify' or 'discover' – in fact, to *invent* – a body of traditional cultural practices, and to celebrate those practices in ways (allegedly scientific and scholarly) which provide an impression of national continuity during a period of rapid social change.

Considered in these terms, the shanty is problematic. Ostensibly the product of a vernacular cultural imagination (and thus available for incorporation within the wider folk revival), at the same time the shanty has a number of properties which militate against the idea of a pristine 'folk' tradition waiting to be discovered in the gaps or on the edges of society. The shanty is 'occasional' – it's generated by the specific occasion of its performances; it's generally improvised (in terms of length and content) to meet the specific requirements of that occasion; it's highly volatile in terms of its national, ethnic and racial content; it's the accidental product of a highly specific conjunction of technology and economics; and, finally, some of its most compelling examples can contain lyrical material that was (and to a large extent still is) categorically repugnant.

In short, the shanty was the product of a residually *oral* culture, rendering it highly resistant to a *literate* critical discourse (such as the one deployed here) whose ideal has always been 'the text'.

*Above: The fully rigged*
Mary L. Cushing, *c.1880.*

*Opposite: Clipper* Three Brothers, *lithograph by Currier & Ives, 1875.*

# 36. STORMALONG JOHN

Oh Stor-my's dead, that good old man, Stor-my-a-long, boys, Storm-a-long John, Oh Stor-my's dead, that good old man, Way-hey-ah, come a-long, get a-long, Stor-my-a-long John

Oh Stormy's dead, that good old man
*Stormy along, boys, Stormalong John*
Oh Stormy's dead, that good old man
*Way hey-ah, come along, get along, Stormy along John*

He slipped his cable off Cape Horn
Close by the place where he was born

We'll dig his grave with a silver spade
His shroud of finest silk was made

We'll lower him down with a golden chain
Each eye will dim with more than rain

I wish I was old Stormy's son
I'd build a ship of a thousand ton

I'd fill her with New England rum
And all my shell-backs they'd have some

For fifty years he sailed the seas
In winter gale and summer breeze

Old Stormy's dead and gone to rest
Of all the sailors he was the best

Old Stormy was a seaman bold
A Grand Old Man of the days of old

**L**aura Smith discerned an African-American influence (derived from the use of the word 'Massa') in the dozen or so shanties relating to the mythical figure of Stormalong John. Both Richard Terry and Captain Whall commended the nobility of this shanty's melody, although the latter's claim that it afforded no improvisation beyond the five verses he gives seems unlikely. In fact, Stan Hugill identified an entire 'family' of Stormalong shanties – related but identifiably different – used for all the main shipboard tasks: capstan, halyards and pumps. (There were also lumberjack and stevedore versions.) He recalled with particular fondness a 'Liverpool' version with verses culled from 'Across the Western Ocean', and the 'hitch' – a wild yelp ('absolutely impossible for a white man to copy', according to Stan) with which his West Indian friend Harding used to sing it.

Echoing Smith, Bert Lloyd suggested that some of the imagery relating to Old Stormy's ceremonial funeral might derive from African-American culture. He also made a connection between Stormalong John and other mythological personages of the sea such as Mother Carey and Davy Jones. Whereas the latter figure has retained his currency (thanks in part to the *Pirates of the Caribbean* franchise), his sometime wife, who functioned as an embodiment of the unforgiving sea in early modern maritime culture, has more or less disappeared from the popular imagination.

The broadcaster and musician Peter Kennedy made the valid point that for a crew to sing about a fine old skipper who's no longer around might have been a subtle way of commenting on the behaviour of their current skipper.

This rousing shanty has numerous alternative titles, including 'Old Stormy', 'Mister Stormalong' and 'Captain Stormalong'. The pumps version I've given here, based on the singing of Ewan MacColl, was just plain 'Stormalong'. I've opted for the present title, however, in honour of the Liverpool shanty group of that name who I heard singing in the Cain's Brewery Tap when I first came to the city in 1987, and whose performances, full of nuance and power, awakened in me a lifelong love of the shanty and all its lore.

Tightening the Tiller Ropes, *illustration from* The Graphic, *18 March, 1871.*

# 37. TOM'S GONE TO HILO

Oh Tom-my's gone, what shall I d-o? A-way you Hi-lo, oh Tom-my's gone and I'll go to-o, Tom's gone to Hi-lo

Oh Tommy's gone, what shall I do?
*Away you Hilo*
Oh Tommy's gone and I'll go too
*Tom's gone to Hilo*

Hilo town is in Peru
It's just the place for me and you

Oh Tommy's gone to Liverpool,
To Liverpool, that Yankee school

Those Yankee sailors you'll see there
With red-top boots and short-cut hair

O Tommy's gone to Baltimore
To dance upon that sanded floor

Tommy's gone to Mobile Bay
To screw down cotton all the day

Tommy's gone to the Rio Grande
To see them girls in the yellow sand

Oh Tommy's gone to Callyo
He'll not come back from there, I know

Oh Tommy's gone to Singapore
I'll never see my Tom no more

The word 'Hilo' retains a flexible range of associations in the series of shanties in which it's deployed – referring as the occasion demands to a settlement in Hawaii or a South American port, a sailors' shindig or a verb of uncertain action. There's also the possibility that it was a mishearing or a mis-transcription of either 'high-low' or 'hello', or indeed 'hell-oh'!

'Tom's Gone to Hilo' was a topsail halyard shanty oriented towards the first of these associations – wherever 'Hilo' (or sometimes 'Ilo') is, that's where Tommy's gone. Captain Whall, Cecil Sharp and John Sampson opt for 'John' and 'Johnny' over 'Tom' and 'Tommy'. All commentators agree that the melody (which they all give slightly different versions of, and which Stan Hugill believed had an oriental touch) is very beautiful. But its aesthetic qualities didn't always translate into shipboard practicality; Hugill tells us that this song 'never found favour with the afterguard, as it took too long to hoist a yard to it on account of the slow and lethargic way in which it was sung by a good shantyman'. Bert Lloyd agrees, writing that 'Tom's Gone to Hilo' was known as 'the mate's anathema' because of the way in which it slowed down the work. He goes on to say that:

...two particular lines of thought seemed to catch the fancy of shantymen when singing the song. One was the conventional theme of parting and absence, usually with ironical references to the behaviour of sweethearts ... Just as often the shantyman would improvise an imaginary voyage to all corners of the globe for wandering Tom.

A third theme emerges from the conjunction of these two: a lament for Tommy's death on the part of his shipmates, or possibly his lover. The stunning version recorded by Gavin Friday and Shannon McNally for the *Son of Rogues Gallery* album certainly gestures in such a direction.

*Illustration* 18th-century sailors *from Charles Rathbone Low's* Her Majesty's Navy, *1890–93.*

# 38. WE'RE ALL BOUND TO GO

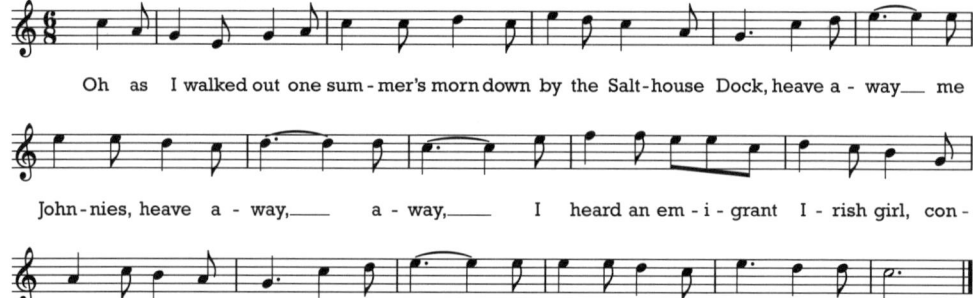

Oh as I walked out one sum-mer's morn down by the Salt-house Dock, heave a-way me John-nies, heave a-way, a-way, I heard an em-i-grant I-rish girl, con-vers-ing with Tap-scott heave a-way me bul-ly boys, we're all bound to go

>Oh as I walked out one summer's morn
>Down by the Salthouse Dock
>>*Heave away me Johnnies, heave away, away*
>I heard an emigrant Irish girl
>Conversing with Tapscott
>>*Heave away me bully boys, we're all bound to go*

'Good morning, Mister
  Tapscott, sir'
'Good morn, my girl,' says he
'And have you got a Packet
  Ship
All bound for Amerikee?'

'Oh yes, I've got a Packet Ship
I have got one or two
I've got the *Jinny Walker*
And I've got the *Kangaroo*'

'I've got the *Jinny Walker*
And today she does set sail
With five and fifty emigrants
And a thousand bags of meal'

The day was fine when we set sail
But night had barely come
And every lubber never ceased
To wish himself at home

It cleared up fine at break of day
And we set sail once more
And every son-of-a-bitch was glad
When we reached Amerikee's
  shore

Bad luck to them Irish sailor boys
Bad luck to them I say
For they all got drunk, and broke
  into me bunk
And stole my clothes away

'Twas at the Castle Gardens
Oh they landed me ashore
And if I marry a Yankee boy
I'll cross the sea no more

But now I'm in New York
And I'm walking through
  the street
With no money in my pockets
And scarce a bit to eat

*On Board an Emigrant Ship* – The Breakfast Bell, *illustration from* The Graphic, *13 September, 1834.*

This popular outward-bound shanty was also known as 'Heave Away, My Johnny'; earlier versions included 'The Irish Emigrant', 'Yellow Meal' and 'Lay Me Down'. The most popular version had lyrical and melodic links with other 'transitional' songs such as 'Across the Western Ocean' and 'The Banks of Newfoundland', while an entirely different version, involving Yankee Pat's arrival in Liverpool for a carouse and his return home again, was popular on American ships.

According to Richard Terry, this version of 'We're All Bound to Go' is one of the few shanties which preserved a definite narrative. In fact, its opening line identifies this song as a kind of narrative 'Come all ye' – a form that emerged in Ireland in the eighteenth century, but came to prominence across Britain with the influx of Irish people into the great industrial centres in the wake of the disastrous famine of the late-1840s. It's also another of those songs (according to Captain Whall, Terry and Stan Hugill) that were sung in an imitative Irish accent (see 'Liverpool Judies', No. 23); and there's also an attempt – with the words 'Amerikee' and 'meal' (pronounced to rhyme with 'mail') – to provide a phonetic rendition of an Irish accent.

Tapscott was an actual shipping agent who operated out of Liverpool between 1842 and 1860. The ship upon which the unfortunate girl sailed was known by many different names in the different versions of this rousing brake-windlass shanty – among others, the *Josey Walker* (Laura Smith), the *Henry Clay* (Whall) and sometimes even the *Dreadnought* (Hugill).

Despite its bouncy rhythm and sunny major key, 'We're All Bound to Go' paints a pretty bleak picture. The warning against shipboard robbery offered by the narrator of 'Across the Western Ocean' is realised in verse seven, while the optimism of the penultimate verse is mitigated in the final one by the reality that awaited many emigrants.

# 39. WHIP JAMBOREE

Whip Jam-bor-ee, Whip Jam-bor-ee, you pig-tail sail-or, hang-ing down be-hind, Whip Jam-bo-ee, Whip Jam-bor-ee Jen-ny get your oat-cakes done

CHORUS:
*Whip Jamboree, Whip Jamboree*
*You pigtail sailor, hanging down behind*
*Whip Jamboree, Whip Jamboree*
*Jenny get your oatcakes done*

Now me lads be of good cheer
For the Irish coast will soon draw near
We'll set a course for the old Cape Clear
Jenny, get your oatcakes done

Now Cape Clear it is in sight
We'll be off Holyhead by tomorrow night
We'll set a course for the old Rock Light
Jenny get your oatcakes done

Now we're passing Fort Perch Rock
All hammocks lashed and the sea-chests locked
We'll wrap her up in the Waterloo Dock
Jenny get your oatcakes done

Now, me lads, we are in dock
We'll be off to Dan Lowrey's on the spot
And there we'll sink a large pint pot
Jenny get your oatcakes done

Now I'm safe upon the shore
I don't give a damn how the winds do roar
I'll drop my anchor, go to sea no more
Jenny get your oatcakes done

But now I've had two weeks ashore
I'll pack my chest, go to sea once more
Bid goodbye to the Liverpool shore
Jenny get your oatcakes done

**A**lso known as 'Whoop Jamboree' (Richard Terry), 'Whup Jamboree' (Douglas Morgan) and sometimes just 'Jamboree' (W.B. Whall), this much-loved homeward-bound shanty was sung at capstan or windlass, although also sometimes used for short hauls. The lyrics that have survived in different versions represent a much-diluted rendering of the original unprintable words. Basically, it seems that the jolly sailor lads are advising their favoured female shore companions to prepare themselves – emotionally, certainly, but principally with reference to their physical disposition – for the homecoming of lovers who have been deprived of amorous activity for the duration of the voyage. Or words to that effect.

Cecil Sharp picked up his version of this shanty from John Short of Watchet. The Liverpool version charts the ship's approach in relation to various famous landmarks: Cape Clear – three miles from the southern Irish coast, and one of the first landfalls looked for by eastward-bound ships; Holyhead – an important port on the western tip of Anglesey; Fort Perch Rock (and its nearby Rock Lighthouse) – built in the 1820s in New Brighton to guard Liverpool against attack by any future Napoleons; Waterloo Dock – designed by famous maritime engineer Jesse Hartley and opened in 1834; and Dan Lowrey's music hall in which many of the great 'artistes' of the day entertained all-comers. The song is a lesson in both geography and history.

I love the idea of the ship passing the half-way point on the trip from New York, with the crew starting to think about arrival in Liverpool and each familiar landmark being ticked off with increasing excitement.

# 40. WHISKY JOHNNY

Oh whis-ky is the life of man, oh whis-ky, John-ny, oh I'll drink whis-ky when I can, whis-ky for me John-ny

Oh whisky is the life of man
*Oh whisky, Johnny*
Oh I'll drink whisky when I can
*Whisky for me Johnny*

Whisky is the life of man
Whisky from an old tin can

Whisky made me pawn my clothes
Whisky gave me this red nose

Whisky here and whisky there
I'd have whisky everywhere

Whisky up and whisky down
Whisky all around the town

I'll drink it hot, I'll drink it cold
I'll drink it new, I'll drink it old

Whisky killed my poor old Dad
Whisky drove my mother mad

Whisky killed my sister Sue
Whisky killed my brother too

If I can't have whisky I'll have rum
That's the stuff to make good fun

Some likes whisky, some likes beer
I wish I had a barrel here

If whisky was a river and I could swim
I'd say here goes and dive right in

Oh whisky straight and whisky strong
Give me some whisky and I'll sing you a song

I thought I heard the Old Man say
Oh whisky for all hands, belay

**A**ll commentators agree that this 'Bacchanalian chant' (Richard Terry) was a prime favourite among the crews, with a multitude of verses to fit whatever task was to hand – halyard, capstan, windlass, pumps. Some of its racier content paused the Victorian collector Laura Smith, who was moved to comment:

[*The*] *sailors' songs are truly characteristic of the men they belong to, and so long as they adapt themselves to the purpose for which they are intended, and help to lighten the labour and regulate the work at sea, we must be content to take them as they are, and not look for drawing-room rose-water sentiment in the ideas that originate and find favour amongst the hard toilers of the briny ocean.*

Good advice, despite which, Laura's broadmindedness in this regard extends no further than rhyming 'whisky' with 'frisky'!

Stan Hugill lists four main variants of 'Whisky Johnny', but it's the first one (included here) – about the virtues and the perils of strong drink – which remains the most popular.[11] Have you ever felt 'groggy'? Or in need of some 'Dutch courage'? Do you prefer a 'dram' or a 'tot' to a glass? If 'yes' to any of these, then you are engaging with a long and deep association between sailors and alcohol. The Royal Navy was still providing daily drams of liquor to its sailors until 1970. The trade-off, it seems, has always been between improved morale, health and courage on the one hand, and the multiple dangers of alcohol abuse on the other – including the potentially fatal danger of a breakdown of discipline.

In the stand-off between whisky's benefits and drawbacks, it's probably fair to say that the latter just about comes out on top. Perhaps we shouldn't be surprised, because whisky was not (according to Hugill) a particularly popular drink among sailors, who had good reason to fear its stupefying effects. Jack's preferred tipples were rum and beer – cheaper, for one thing, and with the added bonus of there being less chance of waking up robbed or shanghaied.

# Stan Hugill: Shantyman and Scholar

Stan Hugill was born in 1906 in the seaside village of Hoylake on the Wirral peninsula, a few miles south of the great port city of Liverpool. His father was a coastguard, and the family lived in a cottage looking out onto the Dee estuary, with a view of the ships approaching and departing Liverpool on the near horizon. Without much formal education, Hugill registered as a sailor, and went to sea in 1921 aged 14. One of the ships upon which he served, a four-masted square-rigger named the *Garthpoole*, was wrecked in 1929. Until the commencement of the Second World War a decade later he served aboard a number of other ships, while also passing a good deal of time ashore in a variety of places around the Pacific rim. He was captured early in the war and spent four years as a German prisoner at the Marlag und Milag Nord camp near Bremen. After repatriation, he spent 25 years as an Outward Bound Instructor in Aberdovey, Wales, while also finding time to take a Diploma in Japanese Studies at the University of London's School of Oriental and African Studies.

It was during this post-war period (and perhaps under the impetus of his newfound taste for formal education) that Stan Hugill turned in earnest to a field with which he was already deeply familiar. After its early-century domination by the rather straitened imagination of collectors such as Cecil Sharp and Richard Runciman Terry, international shanty research was moving into a new phase, and Stan obviously believed he had important ideas and information to impart. Long before the Internet and email, his Aberdovey home became the centre of a great international maritime musical project, with thousands of letters flying back and forth across the seven seas. From the 1950s until the time of his death, Stan Hugill was at the forefront of a growing international shanty movement, contributing to and performing at events across Europe and the United States.

The fruit of all this research is a body of work that thoroughly informs all subsequent engagements with the shanty tradition (including the present one). *Shanties from the Seven Seas* (1961) is a wonderful ragbag of songs and stories. *Sailortown* (1967) represents a key contribution to what has come to be known as 'the blue humanities' (research relating to all matters maritime). *Shanties and Sailors' Songs* (1969) contains the fullest exposition of both the historical background and the functional application of the shanty. *Songs of the Sea* (1977) was a glossy American production with a more internationalist perspective. And finally, some of the articles that Stan contributed to the English folk magazine *Spin* between 1962 and 1973 were collected and posthumously published as *The Bosun's Locker* in 2006. Much of this material is supported by his own wonderfully evocative drawings and maps.

Stan Hugill's reputation as a salty old 'character' should not detract from his achievement as an historian and champion of the shanty. More than any other modern figure, his work laid the basis for ongoing research into the role and function of the shanty as an important practice within the history of international maritime culture. At the same time, he should be celebrated for his implicit appreciation, apparent throughout all his writings, of the power, the joy, and the political significance of communal singing.

*Rigging and sailors,
c.1900, by David de Maus.*

# 1. THE BANKS OF NEWFOUNDLAND

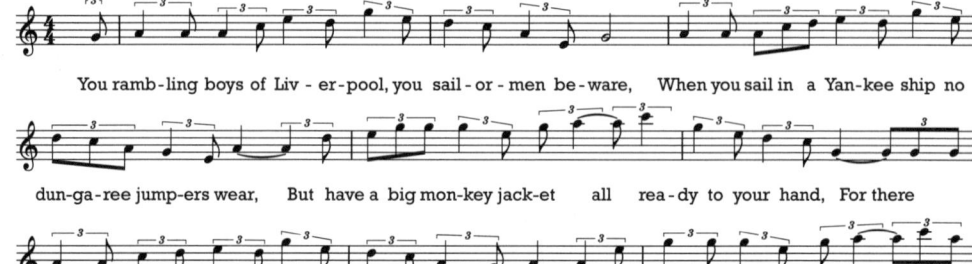

You rambling boys of Liverpool, you sailormen beware
When you sail in a Yankee ship no dungaree jumpers wear
But have a big monkey jacket all ready to your hand
For there blows some cold nor'westers on the Banks of Newfoundland

CHORUS:
We'll scrape her and we'll scrub her with holystone and sand
And we'll think of them cold nor'westers on the Banks of Newfoundland

There was Jack Lynch from Ballynahinch, Mike Murphy and Sam Moore
I tell you well they all suffered like hell on the way to Baltimore
They pawned their gear in Liverpool and they sailed as they did stand
And there blows some cold nor'westers on the Banks of Newfoundland

I dreamed a dream the other night, and thought I was at home
I dreamed that me and my Judy was back in Marybone
We both were in the alehouse with a jug of beer in hand,
But when I woke I found no joke on the Banks of
    Newfoundland.

The mate, he stood on the fo'c'sle head and loudly he did roar
Now rattle her in me lucky lads, we're bound for America's
    shore
Then lay aloft and shake her out and give her all she can stand
For there blows some cold nor'westers on the Banks of
    Newfoundland

So now we're off the Hook, me boys, and the land's all white
    with snow
But soon we'll see the pay table and we'll spend the night
    below
And on the docks, coming down in flocks, those pretty girls
    will stand
Saying it's snugger with me than it is at sea on the Banks
    of Newfoundland

All Hands on Board,
Our Boatswain Cries,
illustration by V. Whall,
1910.

**T**his eighteenth-century transportation ballad slowly metamorphosed into a forebitter on board the transatlantic ships making the hard winter passage from Liverpool to New York described in the lyrics. There are many 'Banks of ...' songs in the folk canon; this one refers not to *river* banks (as do most of them), however, but to the notorious 'Grand Banks' – the extensive series of plateaus found in the shallow waters off Newfoundland. Melville's hero Redburn describes seeing whales there on his first voyage east, as well as a wrecked ship bedecked with dead sailors.

Stan Hugill reiterates the basic point that different kinds of sea song naturally developed different styles of singing. Because it was a work song the shanty placed physical demands on the body, which in turn impacted on performance issues such as breathing, volume, expression, and so on. A different version of 'The Banks of Newfoundland' (with chorus) was often sung at the capstan, but as a forebitter it was invariably sung through the nose in a cod Irish accent, and was full of 'twiddles and quavers' (see the note with No. 23, 'Liverpool Judies').

The lyrics given here combine various versions supplied by Hugill (although not the romantic one featuring 'Bridget Reilly) and the one collected in 1954 by Bert Lloyd from a singing sailor named Ted Howard of Barry, South Wales.

*Opposite:* Holy-Stoning the Deck, *illustration from* James Otis, The Cruise of the Enterprise, *1902.*

*Left: Detail from* The Life of the Naval Sailor, *anonymous print, 1875–1903.*

## 2. CANADEE-I-O

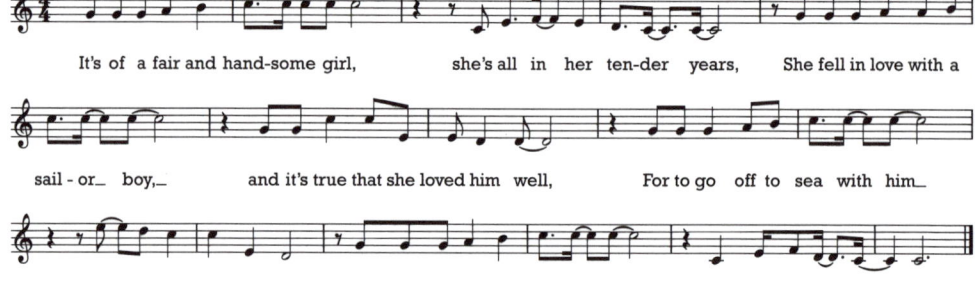

It's of a fair and hand-some girl, she's all in her ten-der years, She fell in love with a sail-or boy, and it's true that she loved him well, For to go off to sea with him like she did not know how, She longed to see that sea-port town called Can-a-dee-i-o

It's of a fair and handsome girl
She's all in her tender years
She fell in love with a sailor boy
And it's true that she loved him well
For to go off to sea with him
Like she did not know how
She longed to see that seaport town called
   Canadee-i-o

So she bargained with the sailor boy
It's all for a piece of gold
Straightaway then he led her
All down into the hold
Saying, 'I'll dress you up in sailor's clothes
Your jacket shall be blue
And you'll see that seaport town called
   Canadee-i-o'

Now, when the other sailors heard the news
Well, they fell into a rage
And with all the ship's company
They were willing to engage
Saying, 'We'll tie her hands and feet, my boys
Overboard we'll throw her
And she'll never see the seaport town of
   Canadee-i-o'

Now, when the captain he heard the news
Well, he too fell into a rage
And with the whole ship's company
He was willing to engage
Saying 'She'll stay in sailor's clothes
Her colour shall be blue
And she'll see that seaport town called
   Canadee-i-o'

Now, when they come down to Canada
Scarcely about half a year
She's married this bold captain
Who called her his dear
She's dressed in silks and satins now
She cuts a gallant show
Finest of all the ladies down in Canadee-i-o

Come, all you fair and tender girls
Wheresoever you may be
I'd have you to follow your own true love
When he goes out on the sea
For if the sailor proves false to you
Well, the captain, he might prove true
You'll see the honour I have gained
By the wearing of the blue

Emigrants Arrival at Cork – A Scene at the Quay, from The London Illustrated News, 10 May, 1851.

Anne Jane Thornton
The Female Sailor,
*anonymous print.*

It should be plain by now that the nineteenth-century merchant marine profession, which provided the context for the emergence of the modern shanty, was almost exclusively masculine. To our modern sensibilities, it was also irredeemably sexist. These facts must figure in any attempt (such as the present one) to retain a positive relationship with the form.

One way in which women did feature in traditional sea-ballad discourse was through the age-old practice of cross-dressing, examples of which may be found in songs such as 'Caroline and Her Young Sailor Bold' and 'The Female Cabin Boy'. In fact, the archive has plenty of examples of women donning men's clothes for one reason or another – all versions, one might say, of the same basic task of trying to empower themselves in a world set up to exploit 'the fairer sex'. Despite this, the patriarchal perspective prevails. In this eighteenth-century English folk song, for example, a young girl dresses as a sailor in order to follow her love to sea; once there, she falls foul of sailor superstition regarding a female presence on board ship, before being rescued, in proper Romantic fashion, by the nearest male authority figure.

There are many ballads and folk songs in which the woman is heard lamenting her ocean-borne lover: the well-known 'Blow the Wind Southerly' is a classic example. 'Canadee-i-o' broaches an alternative perspective on the sea song and the world that produced it.

The version recorded by singer-guitarist Nic Jones for his album *Penguin Eggs* (1980) represents one of the enduring achievements of the modern British folk movement. The score provided here is no more than a gesture towards its complexity and its beauty.

# 3. DO ME AMA

As a sail-or was walk-ing one fine sum-mer day, the squire and the la-dy were mak-ing their way, And the sail-or he heard the squ-ire say "To - night with you I mean to stay with me do - me - a - ma, din - ghy - a - ma, do - me a - ma day"

As a sailor was walking one fine summer day  
The squire and the lady were making their way  
And the sailor he heard the squire say  
'Tonight with you I mean to stay  
With me do-me-ama, dinghy-ama, do-me ama day'

'You must tie a string all around your finger  
With the other end of the string hanging out the  
   window  
And I'll slip by and pull the string  
And you must come down and let me in  
With me do-me-ama, dinghy-ama, do-me ama day'

Says Jack to hisself 'I've a mind to try  
To see if a poor sailor he can win that prize'  
So he stole up and pulled the string  
And the lady came down and she let old Jack in  
With that do-me-ama, dinghy-ama, do-me ama day

Well the squire come by, he was humming a song  
Thinking to himself how it wouldn't be long  
But when he got there no string he found  
Behold his hopes was all dashed to the ground  
With that do-me-ama, dinghy-ama, do-me ama day

Well early next morning, it was just getting light
The lady jumped out of the bed in a terrible fright
For there lay Jack in his tarry old shirt
Behold his face was all covered in dirt
And that do-me-ama, dinghy-ama, do-me ama day

'Oh, what do you want, you tarry sailor
Breaking in a lady's bedroom to steal her treasure?'
'Well now', says old Jack, 'I just pulled the string
And you came down, ma'am, and let me in
With me do-me-ama, dinghy-ama, do-me ama day'

The sailor he says 'Oh forgive me I pray
I'll steal away very quiet at the dawn of the day'
'Oh no', says the lady, 'don't go too far
For I never will part from me Jolly Jack Tar
And that do-me-ama, dinghy-ama, do-me ama day'

This forebitter is based on a ballad entitled 'Jack the Jolly Tar', collected in 1904 by Cecil Sharp from a Mrs Hooper of Hambridge in Somerset. A few years later, Captain Whall included a version entitled 'Doo me Ama' in the first edition (1910) of his collection, suggesting that the transition had already been made from a song *about* a sailor to one that sailors actually sang.

Behind the two-pronged story of a clever working man outfoxing a 'toff', and a 'high' lady falling for a commoner, lie centuries of songs and tales on the same themes – as found, for example, in the *Canterbury Tales*, *The Decameron* and (further afield) *The Arabian Nights*. The Marxist in Bert Lloyd couldn't help but hear 'Do Me Ama' as 'an amiable dream of class revenge'.

Mrs Hooper's original chorus of 'Hey diddley dingo/Hey diddley ding' was replaced in the version collected by Whall (and sung by Lloyd) with the equally nonsensical 'do-me-ama, dinghy-ama, do-me ama day'. Each represents a contribution to the great international musical tradition in which graphic sexual content is described using language that is ridiculous to the sense but quite pleasurable to the ear.

'The Pride of the Ocean',
composed by Thomas E.
Williams, 1852.

# 4. THE DREADNOUGHT

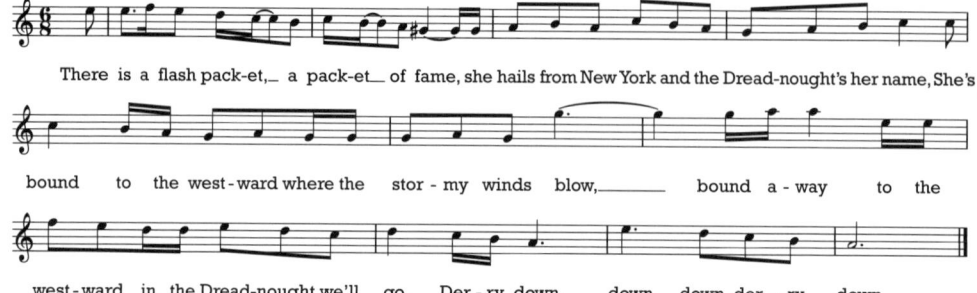

There is a flash packet, a packet of fame,
She hails from New York and the *Dreadnought*'s her name
She's bound to the westward where the stormy winds blow
Bound away to the westward in the *Dreadnought* we'll go
Derry down, down, down derry down

Now the *Dreadnought* she lies in the River Mersey
Awaiting the tug boat to take her to sea
Out around the rock light where the salt tides do flow
Bound away to the westward in the *Dreadnought* we'll go
Derry down, down, down derry down

Now the *Dreadnought*'s a-howling down the wild Irish Sea
Her passengers merry, their hearts full of glee
Her sailors like lions walk the deck to and fro
She's the Liverpool Packet, oh Lord let her go
Derry down, down, down derry down

Now the *Dreadnought*'s arrived in New York once more
So go ashore, shipmates, to the land we adore
With wives and with sweethearts so merry we'll be
And drink to the *Dreadnought* where'ere she may be
Derry down, down, down derry down

Here's a health to the *Dreadnought* and all her brave crew
To brave Captain Samuels, his officers too
Talk about your flash packets, Swallowtail and Black Ball
But the *Dreadnought*'s the flyer that outsails them all
Derry down, down, down derry down

A forebitter that also served on occasion as a capstan shanty, 'The *Dreadnought*' (or '*Dreadnaught*' according to some sources) belongs to a subgenre of sea songs named for the great ships themselves: 'The *Flying Cloud*' (ballad No. 5 in this volume), 'The *Ebenezer*', 'The Good Ship *Kangaroo*', 'The *Irish Rover*', and so forth. The Dreadnought was an American clipper of the Red Cross Line, launched out of Maryport, Massachusetts, in 1853. She served as a packet, operating a regular scheduled service for passengers and freight, and earned the 'flash' sobriquet because of her record-breaking runs between New York and Liverpool.

A different song, 'The *Dreadnought* Mutiny', refers to a famous incident concerning the same ship and a confrontation between the same (American) Captain Samuels and a group of Liverpool-Irish sailors known as the 'Bloody Forty' whose practice it was to ship together in order to protect themselves from 'bucko' mates and masters. Discipline aboard the Western Ocean packets was notoriously severe, as ballads such as 'Andrew Rose' and 'The Cruel Ship's Captain' testify. In this ballad all seems to have ended well, with the crew toasting the captain and his officers after another successful passage. The *Dreadnought* herself wasn't so lucky, however; she sank off Cape Horn in 1869.

Laura Smith's comments in her early collection indicates that 'The *Dreadnought*' was often conflated with the well-known shanty 'Goodbye, Fare-Ye-Well' (see No. 15). The version included here uses the tune of a song lauding the achievements of another New York 'flier': 'The *Dom Pedero*'. When it was sung as a shanty, each verse was followed by a two-line 'bound away' chorus; here we have a quaint 'derry down' refrain which works, I think, better for the soloist than for the ensemble. (This is the way Ewan MacColl sang it on the *The Singing Sailor* in 1955.) For this reason, I've included it here as a 'ballad' rather than a shanty proper.

Dreadnought, *engraving by Jacques La Grange, 1936.*

# 5. THE FLYING CLOUD

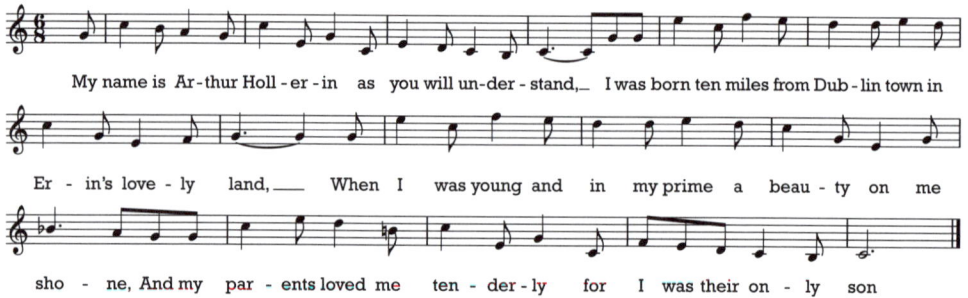

My name is Arthur Hollerin as you will understand
I was born ten miles from Dublin town in Erin's lovely land
When I was young and in my prime a beauty on me shone
And my parents loved me tenderly for I was their only son

My father he bound me to a trade in Waterford's fair town
He bound me to a cooper there by the name of William Brown
I served my master faithfully for seven long years and more
Till I shipped on board the *Erin's Queen* belonging to Tramore

It was on Bermuda's island that I met with Captain Moore
The commander of the *Flying Cloud* from out of Baltimore
He asked me if I'd ship with him a slaving voyage to go
To the burning shores of Africa where the sugar cane does grow

It was after some weeks of sailing we came to Africa's shore
And five hundred of them poor slaves, me boys, from their native land we bore
We marched them up upon a plank and stowed them down below
Just eighteen inches to a man was all they had to go

Then the plague it came and fever too and swept them off like flies
We dragged their bodies up on deck and hove them in the tide
It were better for the rest of them if they had died before
Than to work 'neath the cruel planters in Cuba for evermore

But now our money it is spent, we must go to sea once more
And each man stayed to listen to the words of Captain Moore
'There's gold and silver to be had if with me you'll remain
We'll hoist the pirate flag aloft and scour the Spanish Main'

We plundered many a gallant ship down on the Spanish Main,
Caused many a widow and orphan in sorrow to remain
To the crews we gave no quarter but gave them watery graves
For the saying of our captain was that dead men tell no tales

We ran and fought with many a ship, both frigates and liners too
'Till at last a British Man-O-War, the *Dungemore* hove in view
A shot then killed Captain Moore and twenty of our men
And a bombshell set our ship on fire, we had to surrender then

So it's now to Newgate we are brought, bound down with iron chains
For the sinking and the plundering of ships on the Spanish Main
The judge he found us guilty and we are condemned to die
Young men a warning by me take, lead not such a life as I

So it's fare thee well old Dublin town and the girl I do adore
I'll never kiss your cheek again, I'll squeeze your hand no more
For whisky and bad company have made a wretch of me
Oh young men, a warning by me take and shun all piracy

William Doerflinger makes a case for this long ballad (from which I've omitted a number of verses) being based on the confession of a pirate named Benito de Soto on the eve of his execution in 1829. Although the merchant navy was the product of international capitalism, an alternative economy based on piracy and slavery flourished throughout the Atlantic world well into the nineteenth century, and most sailors would have known (or known somebody who knew) people implicated in that alternative economy.

The mixture of sentimentality and harrowing violence makes this a particularly effective song, and it's no wonder it was a favourite on both British and American ships.

Flying Cloud, *by Jacques La Grange, 1936.*

# (Rock 'n') Roll and Go

Considered in both musical and lyrical terms, the eclectic roots of the shanty extend into many later popular musical genres and forms. Some of the shanty's enduring echoes may, for example, be heard (albeit sometimes in much altered form) in the variety of styles created by the emergence of rock 'n' roll in the 1950s.

This may be to do with the two great musical families sharing a number of common ancestors – an obvious one being the call-and-response format associated with the nineteenth-century work song. This format makes its way into rock 'n' roll via 'the blues', which functions on the one hand as an expression of the existential angst generated by modernity, while at the same time articulating a sense of (a New World African-American) community grounded in oppression and toil. The great river of rock 'n' roll is (to change the metaphor again) also fed by tributaries rising in the Old World; so, while English and Scottish folk song makes an important contribution, Ireland's musical heritage also provides a rich melodic repository from which to borrow and adapt.

Shanties are often associated with pirates, and the latter's enduring popularity (especially among children) is closely linked with the form's continuing currency. The attraction to pirates is cultural, certainly: the clothes, the period, and of course children are drawn to pirates, it seems, for their association with romantic adventure and their outlaw status.[12] And these are in some senses the same values which underpin what might be described as the rock 'n' roll spirit.

Johnny Kidd and the Pirates were 'Shakin' All Over' in 1960. Besides one great song, the band's enduring legacy was to consolidate a trend for the larger-than-life onstage rock persona whose language, behaviour and costume transported them to the edge of 'camp'. In the years since, there has been a good deal of nautically themed popular music; 'sailing' seems to provide a recurring association both with movement (from one environment or state to another) and with escape. There have been fewer overt engagements with the shanty tradition, although one memorable moment was supplied by the Sex Pistols when they recorded (without the contribution of Johnny Rotten) a version of 'The Good Ship Venus' in 1979.

Another London band whose music and image resounded strongly with the shanty was the Pogues. The band's debut album included a raucous 'Sea Shanty' penned by Shane McGowan, as well as a version of the traditional 'Greenland Whale Fisheries'. This was followed by *Rum, Sodomy and the Lash* (1985), a title taken from Winston Churchill's famous description of the British sailor's prospects from a life at sea. In 1987 the Pogues also covered the well-known shanty 'South Australia' as well as a version of 'The *Irish Rover*', the latter memorably performed on *Top of the Pops* with Irish ballad group The Dubliners.

One contemporary English band widely celebrated for their maritime inclinations is The Coral. It might be of interest to note that this band hails from Hoylake on Merseyside, birthplace of the great shanty historian Stan Hugill (and domicile of this volume's author).

*Above:* The great merchantman was captured, *illustration from Frank R. Stockton's* Buccaneers and Pirates of our Coasts, *1898.*

*Opposite:* The boat was run through the surf to the beach, *from Frank R. Stockton, 1898.*

# 6. GO TO SEA ONCE MORE

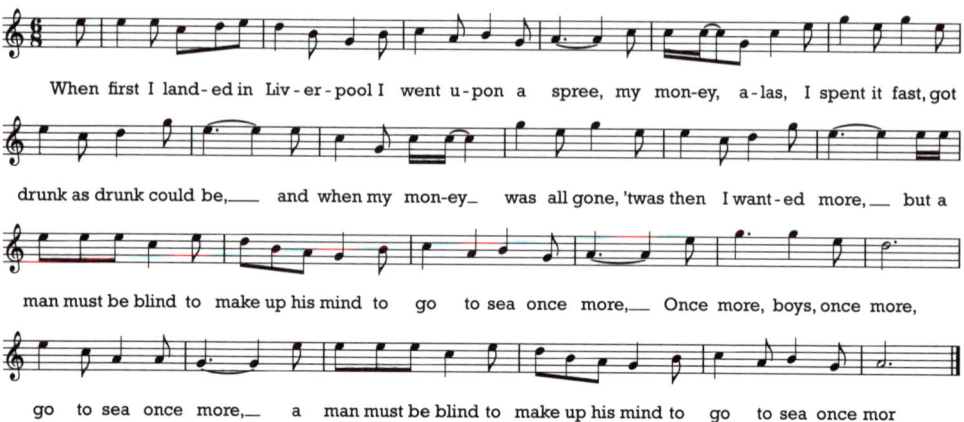

When first I landed in Liverpool I went upon a spree
My money, alas, I spent it fast, got drunk as drunk could be
And when my money was all gone, 'twas then I wanted more
But a man must be blind to make up his mind to go to sea once more

CHORUS:
Once more, boys, once more, go to sea once more
A man must be blind to make up his mind to go to sea once more

I spent the night with Angeline too drunk to roll in bed
Me watch was new and me money too, in the morning with them she'd fled
And as I walked the streets about, the whores they all did roar
There goes Jack Spratt, the poor sailor lad, he must go to sea once more

And as I walked the streets about, I met with the Rapper Brown
I asked him for to take me on and he looked at me with a frown
He said last time you was paid off with me you chalked no score
But I'll give you a chance and I'll take your advance and I'll send you to sea once more

He shipped me on board of a whaling ship bound for the Arctic seas
Where the cold winds blow through the frost and snow and Jamaica rum would freeze
But worse to bear, I'd no hard weather gear for I'd spent all money on shore
'Twas then that I wished that I was dead and could go to sea no more

So come all you bold seafaring men, who listen to me song
When you come off them long trips, I'd have you not go wrong
Take my advice, drink no strong drink, don't go sleeping with them whores
Get married instead and spend all night in bed and go to sea no more

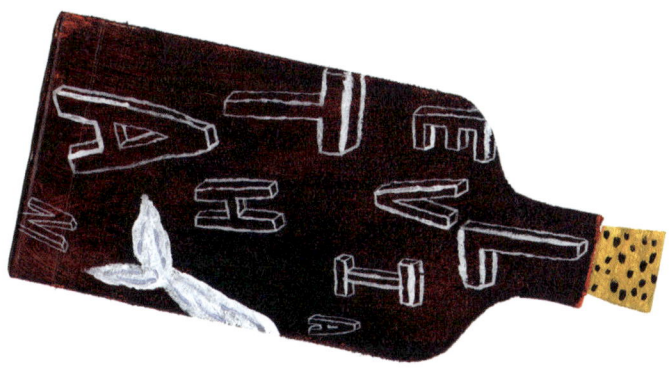

This forebitter was also sung as a capstan shanty, with the last two lines of each verse used as a chorus. An American version, 'Shanghai Brown', is named for one of San Francisco's most notorious crimps. All versions tell the same cautionary tale of a tar who is turned over in port and forced to sign (without the necessary gear) on a whaler. The Arctic reference makes a Liverpool context less likely, although whaling did in fact operate out of that port in the latter half of the eighteenth century.

The version included here is based on the one recorded by The Dubliners in 1968, featuring a lacerating vocal by the great Luke Kelly. A year later, Californian folk rockers The Byrds included a version entitled 'Jack Tarr the Sailor' on their *Ballad of Easy Rider* album – utilising, interestingly enough, the same Liverpool setting rather than the more local one (for them) of San Francisco.

A final piece of trivia: Stan Hugill hears a melodic similarity between 'Go to Sea Once More' and the sixteenth-century song entitled 'Greensleeves'. It's interesting that the same (or similar) melody can cover the delicate sorrows of courtly love as well as the horrors of a sailor's nightmare.

# 7. HIGH BARBAREE

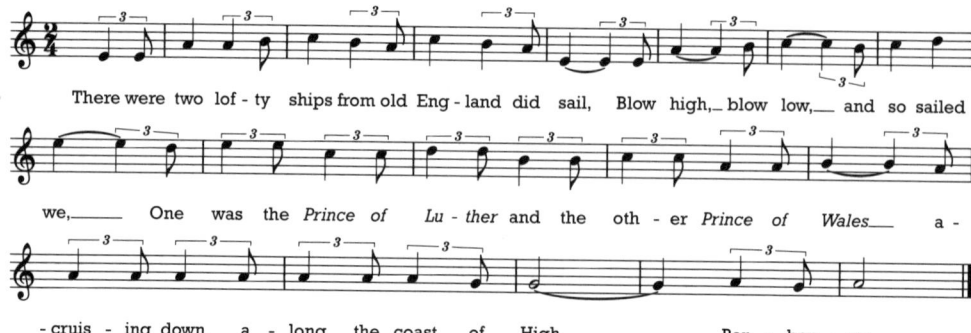

There were two lofty ships from old England did sail
  Blow high, blow low and so sailed we
One was the *Prince of Luther* and the other *Prince of Wales*
  A-cruising down along the coast of High Barbaree

'Aloft there, aloft!' our jolly bosun cried
  'Look ahead, look astern, look a-weather and a-lee'

'There's naught upon the stern, there's naught upon the our lee,
  But there's a lofty ship to windward, and she's sailing fast and free'

'Oh hail her, oh hail her', our gallant captain cried
  'Are you a man-o-war or a privateer?' said he

'Oh, I'm not a man-o-war nor privateer', said he
  'But I'm a salt-sea pirate a-looking for my fee'

'Twas broadside to broadside a long time we lay
  Until the *Prince of Luther* shot the pirate's mast away

'Oh quarter, oh quarter', those pirates they did cry
  But the quarter that we gave them was we sank 'em in the sea

The coast of North Africa was home to the infamous Barbary Corsairs – pirates who terrorised shipping and coastal towns throughout the Mediterranean (and further) during the seventeenth and eighteenth centuries. Rumour of their fierceness, and fear of being captured into their slavery, ran deep through European maritime culture during this period. Much of their income was generated through ransom and 'protection', and their ranks were often swelled by renegade Christians looking for adventure and riches. It was a Dutch captain convert, for example, who led the force that sacked the coastal town of Baltimore (in County Cork) in 1631, carrying off more than 100 local people to a life of slavery – the men as expendable galley slaves, the women as concubines. The historian Linda Colley makes the point that North African slavers would make specific orders for Cornish women and that hundreds, maybe thousands, of people were seized from southwest England and sold in the marketplaces of Morocco and Tunisia.

'High Barbaree' started life as a sixteenth-century song called 'The Sailor's Onely Delight'. A later broadside version may be found in both the Roxburghe and Child collections. With different melodies the song retained its shipboard popularity right down to the end of the nineteenth century.

John Sampson includes 'High Barbaree' in his 'Capstan Shanties' section, but admits in his notes that it was not very well known as a work song. Stan Hugill recalled a version entitled 'The Salcombe Seaman' sung at the capstan. The song's solo-refrain structure doesn't preclude a shanty version, but it seems everywhere to have functioned as a forebitter telling a coherent story of the defeat of a North African pirate by two ships of the Royal Navy.

Sampson gives 'so *say* we' in the first refrain, but I've stuck with the 'so *sailed* we' version given by both Captain Whall and Hugill. The second refrain may be scanned without the 'a-cruising', and the two versions tend to be alternated in practice.

The pirates climbed up the sides of the man-of-war as if they had been twenty-nine cats, *from Frank R. Stockton's* Buccaneers and Pirates of our Coasts, *1898.*

# 8. THE LEAVING OF LIVERPOOL

Fare thee well to Prince's Landing Stage, River Mersey fare-thee-well, I am bound for California, it's a place that I know right well, So fare thee well, my own true love, when I return united we will be, It's not the leaving of Liverpool that grieves me but me darling when I think of thee

Fare thee well to Prince's Landing Stage
River Mersey fare-thee-well
I am bound for California
It's a place that I know right well

CHORUS:
So fare thee well, my own true love
When I return united we will be
It's not the leaving of Liverpool that grieves me
But me darling when I think of thee

Oh I'm bound to California
By way of the stormy Cape Horn
I expect that I will curse the day
And the hour that I was born

I am bound on a Yankee clipper ship
*Davy Crockett* is her name
And the Captain's name is Burgess
And they say that she's a floating hell

It's my second trip with Burgess in the *Crockett*
And I think I know him well
If a man's a seaman, he can get along
But if he's not then he's sure in hell

So fare-well Lower Frederick Street
Anson Terrace, and Park Lane
I think it will be some long time
Before I see you again

Oh I am bound away to leave you
Goodbye, my love, goodbye
And there's but one thing that grieves my mind
And it's leaving you behind

This ballad originated in the nineteenth century, although it seems to have disappeared from the record until it was published by the American collector William Doerflinger in his *Shantymen and Shantyboys* (1951). Doerflinger actually collected separate versions from two retired sailors in New York (one in 1938, one in 1942), one of which seems to have served as a capstan shanty. Either way, its reappearance was just in time to catch the folk movement that was taking off in the United States, whence it spread back across 'the pond' to become probably the most famous 'Liverpool' song in existence.

Adaptations and versions abound. After it was recorded by Ewan MacColl in 1962, versions followed by successful groups such as The Dubliners and the Clancy Brothers and Tommy Makem, as well as Liverpool's premier folk group The Spinners. In his early 1960s magpie period, Bob Dylan produced a version called simply 'Farewell' – the irony being that he had to go to London to hear a version of the original. A few years later the Canadian singer-songwriter Tom Paxton 'borrowed' parts of the melody for his international hit 'The Last Thing on My Mind'.

This ballad has always been particularly popular in Ireland, perhaps as a result of the fact that Liverpool, being as it was a primary departure point for emigrants, loomed so large within the Irish cultural imagination. The song's familiarity can obscure the pathos, indeed the tragedy, of the lyric. There's a sense in which it's difficult, if not impossible, to 'hear' 'The Leaving of Liverpool', and thus to respond to the agony of separation that it relates.

Launched out of Mystic, Connecticut, in 1853, the *David Crockett* made frequent voyages between Liverpool and California under the command of Captain John Burgess. The poor captain, it seems, was lost overboard in 1874.

*Overleaf: Plan of Liverpool by J Rapkin, 1845. Vignettes include the Sailors' Home (bottom right).*

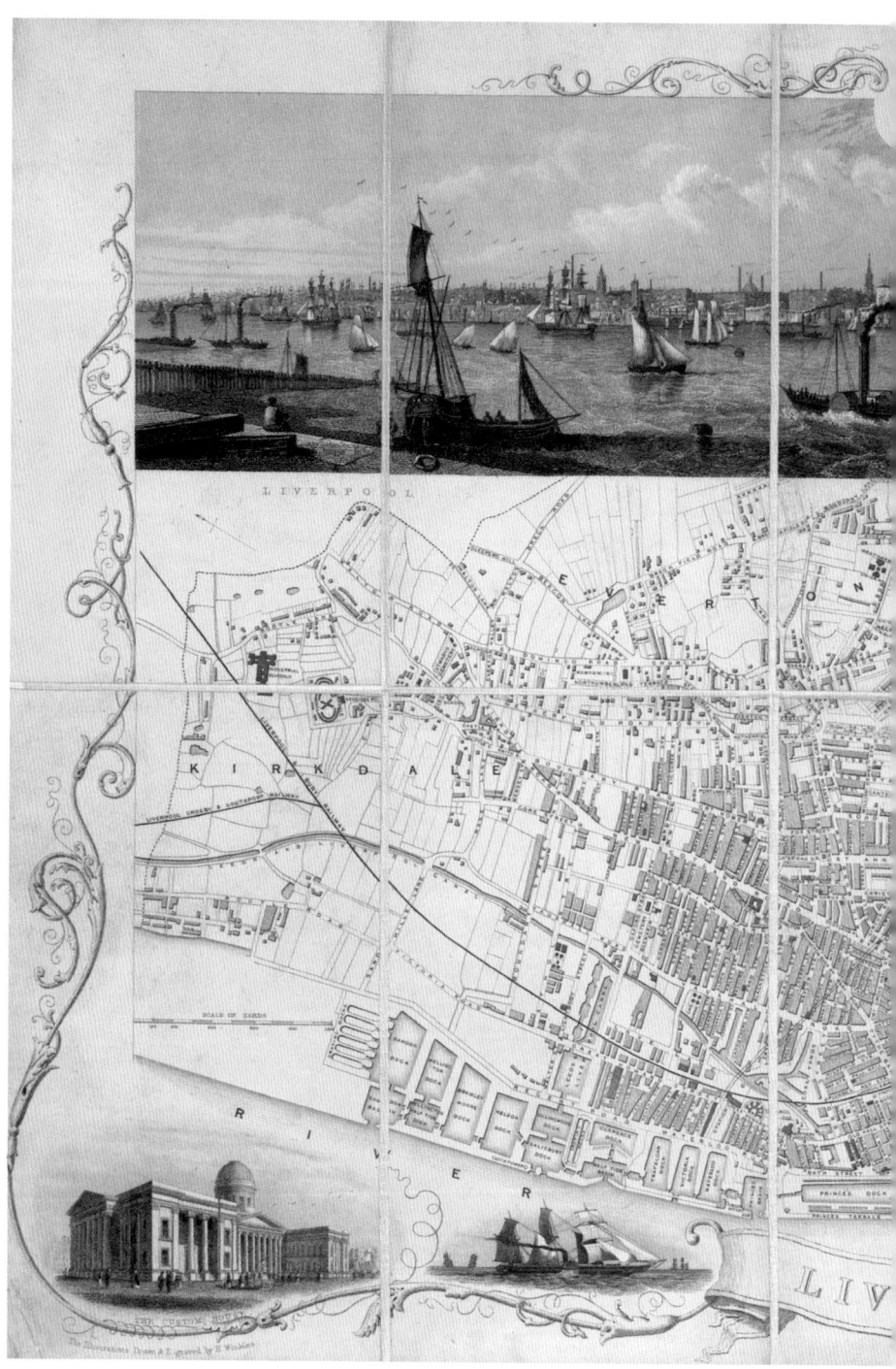

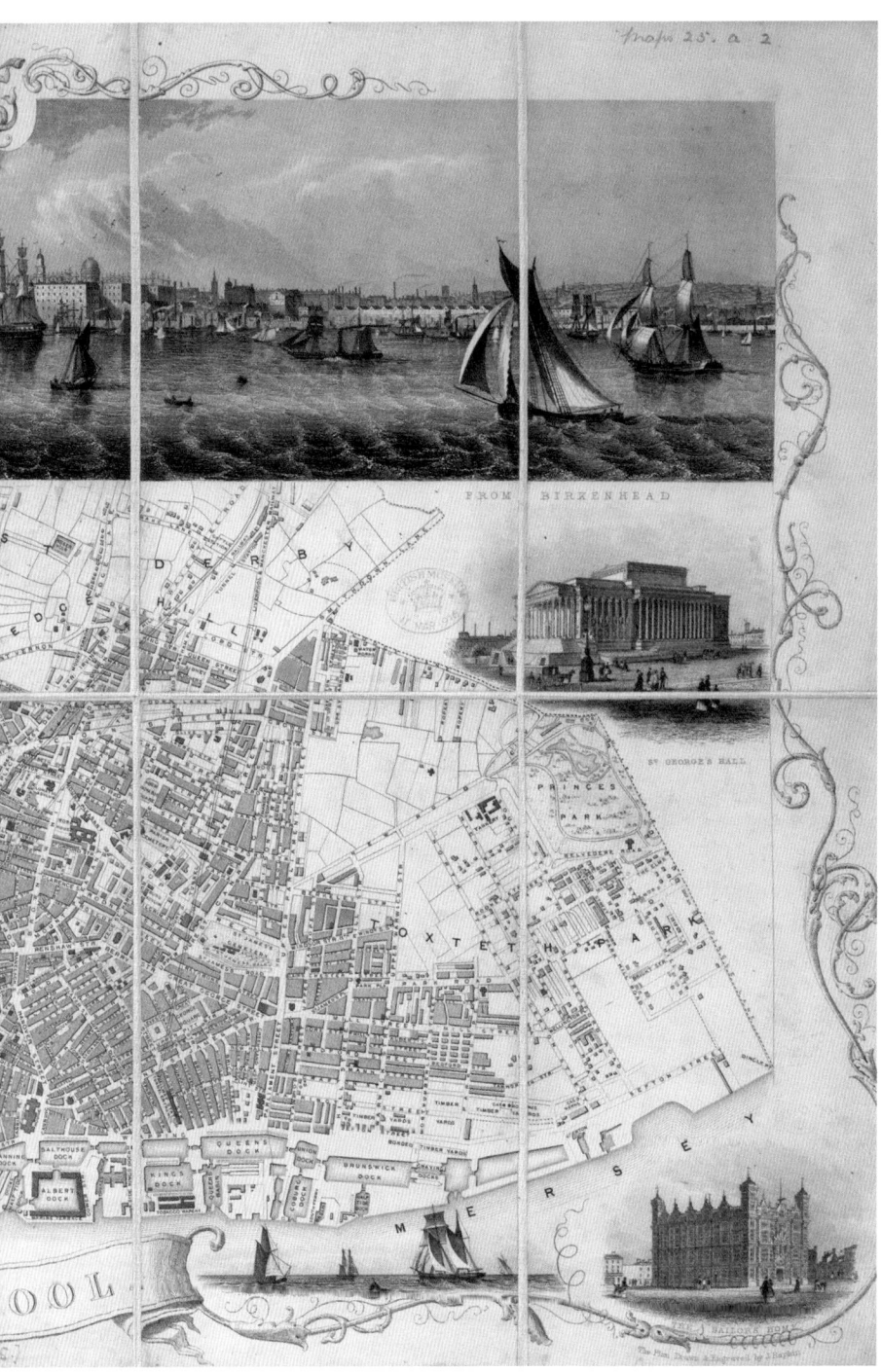

# 9. MAGGIE MAY

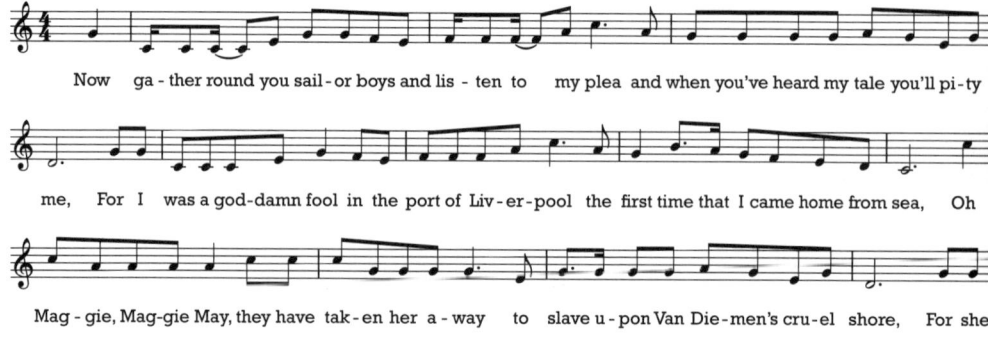

Now gather round you sailor boys and listen to my plea
And when you've heard my tale you'll pity me
For I was a goddamn fool in the port of Liverpool
The first time that I came home from sea

CHORUS:
Oh, Maggie, Maggie May, they have taken her away
To slave upon Van Diemen's cruel shore
For she robbed so many whalers, and many a drunken
   sailor
But she'll never cruise down Lime Street any more

I paid off at the Home from a voyage to Sierra Leone
Two pound ten a month had been my pay
When I drew the tin I grinned, but I very soon got skinned
By a girl with the name of Maggie May

I won't forget the day when I first met Maggie May
She was cruising up and down old Canning Place
With a figure so divine like a frigate of the line
So me, being a sailor, I gave chase

Next day I woke in bed, with a sore and aching head
No shoes or shirt or trousers could I find
I asked her where they were, and she answered,
    'My dear sir,
They're down in Kelly's knock-shop, number nine'

Oh, that thieving Maggie May, she robbed me of my pay
When I slept with her last night ashore
And the judge he guilty found her of robbing a
    homeward-bounder
Now, she'll never roll down Park Lane any more

She was chained and sent away from Liverpool next day
The lads all cheered as she rolled down the bay
And every sailor lad he only was too glad
They sent that old whore down to Botany Bay

**L**ike many people of a certain age, the first time I heard this song was as an outtake sung by John Lennon between tracks on *Let It Be*, that sad album documenting the disintegration of The Beatles. That was entirely appropriate, of course, because it's a song whose roots sink deeply into Liverpool's maritime heritage. Park Lane, for example, is only a short distance from the Paradise Street that features in 'Blow the Man Down', while the Sailors' Home referenced in the second verse was established in Canning Place in 1850 to provide an alternative to the depredations of Sailortown.[13]

Stan Hugill tells us that 'Maggie May' served as a capstan shanty, but most commentators identify it as a forebitter. It tells a familiar tale of the sailor, the whore and the robbery – the variation being that the eponymous heroine in this instance is captured and transported to Australia.

Writing in the late-1950s, Hugill observed that a version of the song 'still survives in a mangled form in Liverpool even today', where it was performed by the Viper Skiffle Group. I wonder was it also sung by that other skiffle group, The Quarrymen, as seen in *Nowhere Boy* (2009), Sam Taylor-Wood's film of the early life of John Lennon?

*Above:* Liverpool Docks, from The Earth and its Inhabitants *by Élisée Reclus, 1881.*

*Opposite:* Lightning, *engraving by Jacques La Grange, 1936.*

# 10. SPANISH LADIES

Fare-well and a-dieu to you fair Span-ish lad-ies, fare-well and a-dieu you lad-ies of Spain, For we've re-ceived or-ders to sail for old Eng-land but we hope ver-y short-ly to see you a-gain

CHORUS:
Farewell and adieu to you fair Spanish ladies
Farewell and adieu you ladies of Spain
For we've received orders to sail for old England
But we hope very shortly to see you again

We'll rant and we'll roar like true British sailors
We'll rant and we'll rave across the salt sea
Till we strike soundings in the channel of Old England
From Ushant to Scilly is thirty-four leagues

We hove our ship to, with the wind at sou'west, boys
We hove our ship to for to take soundings clear
In fifty-five fathoms with a fine sandy bottom
We filled our main topsail, up Channel did steer

The first land we made was a point called the Deadman
Next Ramshead off Plymouth, Start, Portland and Wight
We sailed by Beachy, by Fairlee and Dover
Then bore straightaway for the South Foreland Light

Then the signal was made for the Grand Fleet to anchor
We clewed up our topsail, struck out tacks and sheets
We stood by our stoppers, we brailed in our spankers
And anchored ahead of the noblest of fleets

*Tars Carousing, illustration by George Cruikshank, from Charles Dibden, 1841.*

Let every man here drink up his full bumper
Let every man here drink down his full bowl
And let us be jolly and drown melancholy
Singing here's a good health to all true-hearted souls

**W**e finish with one of the most well-liked and widely dispersed of sea songs. 'Spanish Ladies' started life as a Royal Navy ballad, but also proved popular in the merchant service where, although featuring principally as a forebitter, it was employed on occasion as a capstan shanty. It was also widely known as 'Farewell and Adieu' (and variants thereon), and there are adaptations in the sea-music traditions of many nations. Like 'Whip Jamboree', the verses track the homeward journey through the identification of familiar landmarks – this time, in the English Channel: 'Deadman', 'Ramshead' and 'Fairlee' were sailor names for the Dodman Point near Plymouth, Rameshead and Fairlight Hill near Hastings.

John Sampson believed that such familiarity with sailor parlance, as well as the use of technical language in some of the versions, indicates a proper sailor composition rather than a landsman's effort. Captain Whall, meanwhile, disdained the modern major key version of 'Spanish Ladies', which although livelier and faster than the minor one had (he claimed) none of its character. It's that characterful minor version that is given here.

The first time I ever heard 'Spanish Ladies' was when the actor Robert Shaw, playing Quint the shark-hunter, sang a version in *Jaws*.

# The Shanty Today

Each year there are shanty and maritime music festivals in port towns and cities across the world: France, Germany, Netherlands, Denmark, Australia – anywhere with a maritime heritage that might prove interesting or attractive to locals and tourists.

The International Sea Song Festival Shanties (the translator was obviously a literalist) in land-locked Krakow taps into the form's enduring popularity in Poland, where there is a progressive scene pushing the shanty in directions guaranteed to make the purists wince. The biggest dedicated event in Britain is the annual Falmouth International Sea Shanty Festival, which has run in June every year since 2011, and which in 2019 featured 66 artists from every part of the world. North America also has a number of large, dedicated annual events, such as the festivals in San Diego and Québec. Events like these are typically integrated into the region's wider tourist provision.

The 'Glastonbury of shanties', however, is the Seaport Sea Music Festival held annually at the Seaport Museum in Mystic, Connecticut, in the United States since 1979. The event attracts not only a great range of performers but also a variety of researchers interested in different aspects of the shanty tradition. (The 'blue humanities' mentioned earlier have proved especially popular in American academia.) 'Museum' is perhaps a misleading word for what is an incredibly vibrant institution, and the music festival is in fact only one of a range of educational and outreach activities dedicated to exploring and maintaining the USA's immensely rich maritime heritage.

Besides these dedicated events, most contemporary British folk festivals (including the major annual ones in Cambridge, Sidmouth and Shrewsbury) also feature prominent maritime 'strands' – a great range of sea-themed music up to and including the shanty. Two of the higher-profile artists who have tapped a shanty 'vibe' in recent years include Bellowhead and Seth Lakeman – the first, an ever-evolving ensemble looking to

establish English folk music as part of the country's musical soundscape; the second, a multi-instrumentalist songwriter from Devon whose home-produced album *Kitty Jay* was shortlisted for the prestigious Mercury Music Prize in 2005. To these should be added Port Isaac's Fisherman's Friends whose eponymous 2010 album of (mostly) traditional shanties reached No. 9 in the UK Albums Chart, and who briefly raised the form's national profile. A film focusing on how the album came to be made went on general release in 2019.

The 2010s also saw the emergence into the mainstream of the 'hipster' subculture – recurring elements of which include a taste for microbrewery beer, speciality coffee, artisan bread, vintage clothing (preferably acquired cheaply from the charity shop), veganism and high-visibility tattoos. This period also witnessed the return of the full beard as an expression of a more authentic masculinity. Not all of these trends are relevant, of course, but some resonate clearly with what might be described as a residual maritime aesthetic – one important element of which is the shanty itself. And while, in musical terms, there's no obvious connection between the shanty and the hipster lifestyle, the latter's penchant for authenticity and a kind of artisinal masculinity certainly establishes a space for potentially fruitful encounters.

Above: Heaving the Lead, *from Charles Rathbone Low's* Her Majesty's Navy, *1890–93.*

Opposite: Marine Artilleries.1862, *anonymous illustration of a Spanish naval uniform, 1910.*

# GLOSSARY

The sea looms irresistibly large in human history and has generated a sizeable lexicon of terms and phrases. The following are some of the lesser-known words that crop up in the songs included in this volume. Besides Stan Hugill's useful lists, I've relied heavily on C.W.T. Layton's *Dictionary of Nautical Words and Terms* (1955), revised by Peter Clissold (Glasgow: Brown, Son and Ferguson, 1987).

**advance** An order for a month's wages, paid to sailors when they signed on, the advance-note was intended to purchase necessities for the voyage, but too often ended up in the alehouse and the brothel.

**aloft** Retaining a variety of meanings, according to Layton, but mostly referring to the highest part of the upper deck.

**bar** A bank across the entrance to a harbour, acting as a breakwater.

**Barbary Coast** The name given by Europeans to the coast of North Africa, comprising parts of modern-day Morocco, Algeria, Libya, Morocco and Tunisia. It was home to the 'Barbary Pirates' who terrorised the Mediterranean and Atlantic coast from the sixteenth to the nineteenth centuries.

**barque** A word with a complex nautical etymology, but typically refers to a sailing ship with three or more masts.

**beef-kid** A galley utensil for carrying meat from the coppers.

**belay** To make fast a rope by tying it off; often used to mean stop or cancel.

**bilges** Spaces by the side of the vessel into which excess water ran, and from which such water could be drained by using a 'bilge pump'.

**bosun** Also bos'n and boatswain; in the merchant navy it refers to a trustworthy and experienced petty officer who is the foreman of the crew.

**The Bowery** A tough neighbourhood in southern Manhattan, notorious (in the latter nineteenth century) for vice and violence.

**bowline** A rope leading from the deck to the edge of a sail when the vessel is underway.

**bucko** A bullying officer.

**Callyo** The port of Callao, the port district of Lima, Peru.

**canny** Shrewd and well-organised.

**Cape Stiff** Alternative sailor name for Cape Horn.

**capstan** A barrel-shaped machine used for heaving in ropes and chains.

**crimp** A person who profits from a sailor by robbery (in many forms) or by procuring his labour through trickery or coercion.

**crossing the line** Sailing across the equator.

**donkey** A small steam engine used for shipboard tasks, thus reducing the number of men required; can also refer to a heavy jacket.

**flash** Fast and smart when applied to the packet ships; a 'flashman' usually referred to a pimp, a 'flash girl' to a prostitute.

**flippers** Hands.

**fly** Knowing and clever.

**flying-fish sailor** A mariner who preferred to work the warmer Asiatic routes.

**fo'c'sle head** The forecastle head; merchant navy name for topgallant forecastle.

**fore peak** The space between the forward collision bulkhead and the ship's central wooden spine.

**Frisco** Slang for San Francisco.

**galley** Onboard compartment for the preparation and cooking of food.

**growl** Complain.

**guano** The accumulated excrement of seabirds and bats, used as fertiliser and for explosives.

**halyards** 'Halliards', the ropes by which sails are hoisted.

**holystone** White sandstone used to scrub a wooden deck.

**jamboree** A large boisterous party.

**Jack** Slang name for a sailor.

**Judy** Slang name for a young woman, especially common in Liverpool.

**knight heads** Strong timbers (usually oak) central to the construction of wooden vessels.

**leach** The edge of a square sail.

**Limejuice sailor** Description of British sailors, following the introduction of citrus fruit onboard British ships in the late eighteenth century to combat scurvy.

**lubber** Clumsy and unskilled person lacking knowledge of the sea.

**luff** The weather side of any sail or vessel; opposite to 'lee'.

**mainsail** The principal sail.

**mate** Senior officer assistant to the captain, responsible for important duties relating to work rota and navigation.

**Mobile Bay** Important American cotton port on the Gulf of Mexico, one of the principal places for the composition and evolution of shanties.

**Old Man** Fond term for the captain.

**packet rat** A 'packet' was initially a mail ship that also carried passengers and cargo, but came over time to refer to a passenger vessel on a regular run. A 'packer rat' was one of the tough sailors regularly employed on one of the early to mid-nineteenth-century ships running between Liverpool, New York and Boston.

**pannikin** A small metal drinking cup.

**Paradise Street** A street on the edge of Liverpool's Sailortown.

**pawl** A short, pivoted metal bar with a shaped toe used as part of the capstan (and later windlass) function.

**pumps** Device (multi-part and of diverse design) for clearing the vessel of accumulated water.

**quarterdeck** Upper deck running back from the main mast.

**Rio Grande** Not (according to Hugill) the river in Mexico, but the one further south in Brazil, surrounded by sand dunes and the site of an eighteenth-century gold rush.

**roll and go** A phrase with multiple associations and applications, one of which might be 'prepare for departure'.

**rough and tumble** One of countless euphemisms for sex.

**royal yard** The upper sail of a square-rigged ship.

**saltpetre** A naturally occurring form of sodium nitrate (sometimes used as a preservative or curing agent) found in regions of Chile and Peru.

**scuppers** Holes in a vessel's bulwark (waterway) allowing water to flow off.

**shellback** An old and experienced sailor.

**skyhoot** Variation on 'scoot'?

**skysail** High-set square sail.

**slipped his cable** Euphemism for died.

**tar** Colloquial name for a sailor, although rarely applied (according to Layton) to a merchant seaman.

**tin** Generic name for cash.

**topgallant forecastle** The short, raised deck at the front of the vessel.

**Vallipo** Sailor nickname for the port of Valparaiso in Chile.

**Western Ocean, western sea** The Atlantic.

**windlass** A machine used for working cable, powered originally by hand, subsequently by steam or electricity.

**yardarm** The outer end of a yard (a spar fitted across a mast), from which mutineers were hung.

# FURTHER READING AND LISTENING

## READING

Atkinson, David. *An Introduction to English Sea Songs and Shanties*. British Council, London, 2016.

Boyes, Georgina. *The Imagined Village: Culture, Ideology and the English Folk Revival*. (Originally published 1993.) No Masters Co-operative, Leeds, rev. ed. 2010.

*The Clancy Brothers and Tommy Makem Song Book*. Oak Publications, New York, 1964.

Colcord, Joanna C. *Roll and Go*. Heath Cranton, London, 1924.

Doerflinger, William M. *Shantymen & Shantyboys: Songs of the Sailor & Lumberman*. Macmillan, New York, 1951.

Frank, Stuart M. *Sea Chanteys and Sailors' Songs: An Introduction for Singers and Performers, and a Guide for Teachers and Group Leaders*. Kendall Whaling Museum Monograph No. 11, Sharon, Massachusetts, 2000.

Greenleaf, Elizabeth B. and Mansfield, Grace Y. *Ballads and Sea-Songs of Newfoundland*. Harvard University Press, Cambridge, Massachusetts, 1933.

Hamilton-Paterson, James. *Seven-Tenths: The Sea and its Thresholds*. (Originally published 1992.) Faber & Faber, London, 2007.

Hanley, James. *Sailor's Song*. Nicholson & Watson, London, 1943.

Harker, Dave. *One for the Money: Politics and Popular Song*. Hutchinson, London, 1980.

*Fakesong: The Manufacture of British Folk Song, 1700 to the Present Day*. Open University Press, Milton Keynes, 1985.

Healy, James N. *Irish Ballads and Songs of the Sea*. Mercier Press, Cork, 1967.

Hobsbawn, Eric and Ranger, Terence. (eds.) *The Invention of Tradition*. (Originally published 1983.) Cambridge University Press, Cambridge, 2010.

Hugill, Stan. *Shanties from the Seven Seas: Shipboard Work-songs and Songs Used as Work-songs from the Great Days of Sail*. (Originally published 1961.) Mystic Seaport, Mystic, Connecticut, 1994.

*Sailortown*. Routledge & Kegan Paul, London, 1967.

*Shanties and Sailors' Songs*. Herbert Jenkins, London, 1969.

*Songs of the Sea: The Tales and Tunes of Sailors and Sailing Ships*. McGraw-Hill, New York, 1977.

*The Bosun's Locker: Collected Articles 1962–1973*. David Herron Publishing, Todmorden, Yorkshire, 2006.

Legman, Gershon. *The Horn Book: Studies in Erotic Folklore and Bibliography*. (Originally published 1963.) Cape, London, 1970.

Linebaugh, Peter and Rediker, Marcus. *The Many-Headed Hydra: Sailors, Slaves, Commoners, and the Hidden History of the Revolutionary Atlantic*. Verso, London, 2000.

Lloyd, A.L. *Folk Song in England*. (Originally published 1967.) Panther, London, 1969.

Masefield, John. (ed.) *A Sailor's Garland*. Methuen & Co., London, 1906.

Melville, Hermann. *Redburn: His First Voyage. Being the Sailor-boy Confessions and Reminiscences of the Son-of-a-Gentleman, in the Merchant Service*. (Originally published 1849.) Penguin, London, 1986.

*Moby-Dick; or, The Whale*. (Originally published 1851.) Penguin, London, 2003.

Morgan, Douglas. (ed.) *What Do You Do with a Drunken Sailor? Unexpurgated Sea Shanties*. Echo Point Books & Media, Brattleboro, Vermont, 2013.

Proctor, David. *Music of the Sea*. HMSO, London, 1992.

Roud, Steve. *Folk Song in England*. Faber & Faber, London, 2017.

Roud, Steve and Bishop, Julia. (eds.) *The New Penguin Book of English Folk Songs*. (Originally published 2012.) Penguin, London, 2014.

Runcie, Charlotte. *Salt on Your Tongue: Women and the Sea*. Canongate, Edinburgh, 2019.

Sampson, John. *The Seven Seas Shanty Book*. Boosey & Co., London, 1927.

Sharp, Cecil J. (ed.) *A Book of British Song for Home and School*. John Murray, London, 1902.

*English Folk-Chanteys*. Simpkin, Marshall, Hamilton, Kent & Co., London, 1914.

Smith, Laura Alexandrine. *The Music of the Waters: A Collection of the Sailors' Chanties, or Working Songs of the Sea, of All Maritime Nations. Boatmen's, Fishermen's, and Rowing Songs, and Water Legends*. Keegan Paul, Trench & Co., London, 1888.

# NOTES

Gerry Smyth, 'Shanty-Singing and the Irish Atlantic: Identity and Hybridity in the Musical Imagination of Stan Hugill' in Milne, Graeme and Tackley, Catherine (eds.), *A Special Edition of the International Journal of Maritime History*, 29(2), 2017, 387–406.

Terry, Richard Runciman. *The Way of the Ship: Sailors, Shanties and Shantymen*. (Originally published, Vol.I, 1921; Vol.II, 1926.) Fireship Press, Tucson, Arizona, 2008.

Vaughan Williams, Ralph and Lloyd, A.L. (eds.) *The Penguin Book of English Folk Songs*. (Originally published 1959.) Penguin, London, 1969.

Whall, W.B. *Sea Songs and Shanties*. (Originally published 1910.) James Brown & Son, Glasgow, (5th edition) 1926.

## LISTENING

The Albion Band, *Rise Up Like the Sun*. Harvest, 1978.
Bellowhead, *Matachin*. Navigator Records, 2008.
Fisherman's Friends, *Port Isaac's Fisherman's Friends*. Universal Records, 2010.
Nic Jones, *Penguin Eggs*. Topic Records, 1980.
Seth Lakeman, *Kitty Jay*. Seth B. Lakeman, 2004.
A.L. Lloyd and Ewan MacColl, *The Singing Sailor*. Topic Records, 1954.
*Short Sharp Shanties* at http://www.umbermusic.co.uk/SSSnotes.htm#shanties
The Spinners, *Maggie May: The Best of The Spinners*. Pulse, 1977.
Various, *Blow the Man Down: A Collection of Sea Songs and Shanties*. Topic Records, 1993.
Various, *Farewell Nancy*. Topic Records, 1964.
Various, *Rogue's Gallery: Pirate Ballads, Sea Songs & Chanteys*. ANTI, 2006.
*Son of Rogues Gallery: Pirate Ballads, Sea Songs & Chanteys*. ANTI, 2013.
Various, *Sailors' Songs & Sea Shanties: A Classic Collection of Sea Songs & Shanties in Authentic Performances*. (Originally released 1957.) Re-released Topic Records, 1971; 2004.
Various, *Sea Songs and Shanties: Traditional English Sea Songs and Shanties from the Last Days of Sail*. Saydisc, 1994.

1 Captain Whall and John Sampson link 'A-Roving' to a song included in Thomas Heywood's *The Rape of Lucrece* (1608). Although Stan Hugill disputes this connection, echoes may certainly be heard in the poetry of writers such as Burns, Byron and Masefield (who described it as one of the most beautiful of all shanty melodies), as well as in a host of folk and popular songs from all parts of the world.

2 The debate is irresolvable at this stage, but Richard Terry makes a fair point: '…if the sailor … did seize on "Camptown Races" because of its amazing popularity, why did he not seize on any other songs of Foster ("Swanee River" for instance) which had a greater vogue and were equally adaptable as shanties?'

3 During the successful *Pirates of the Caribbean* franchise in the 2000s, the American film star Johnny Depp became interested in shanties and commissioned an album – entitled *Rogue's Gallery* (2006) – featuring a variety of pirate songs, sea ballads and shanties performed by some of his musical friends, including Bono, Nick Cave, Bryan Ferry, Eliza Carthy, Lucinda Williams, Jarvis Cocker and Lou Reed. A second album, *Son of Rogues Gallery*, followed in 2013, featuring contributions from an equally stellar line-up, including Shane McGowan, Beth Orton, Tom Waits, Keith Richards, Iggy Pop, Macy Gray, Patti Smith, Michael Stipe, Frank Zappa, Courtney Love and Marianne Faithfull. Listening to these interpretations, one is struck by both the extent and the profundity of the shanty's influence on so much of modern popular music.

4 Stan Hugill identifies six major variants of the outward-bound capstan shanty entitled 'Rio Grande', for example: 1) 'Leaving Liverpool'; 2) 'Gold Rush' version; 3) 'The Milkmaid'; 4) 'Leaving New York'; 5) 'The Fishes'; and 6) 'The Mail'.

5 Dan Lowrey was an impresario in the early days of music hall. The following description comes from R.J. Broadbent's *Annals of the Liverpool Stage* (Edward Howell, Liverpool, 1908): 'The Malakoff Music Hall was brought into existence during the 'fifties, by the late Dan Lowrey. It was situated in Cleveland Square and was a popular resort for youthful and ancient mariners. In addition to variety performances, plays and pantomimes were also submitted. In one of Mr. Lowrey's advertisements (1864), he amusingly stated that there is "a private box for captains *and gentlemen*." Outside the Malakoff there is a statue of Mr. Lowrey in one of his favourite Irish characters. The building is still in existence.'

6 Laura Smith has 'Haulin' the Bowline'; John Sampson has 'Hauling on the Bowline'; Danny Spooner used to sing 'Haul in the Bowline'; and Stan Hugill moves blithely between 'Hauling on the Bowline', 'Haul on the Bowline', 'Haul the Bowline' and 'Haul Away the Bowline'.

7 Such delicacy doesn't extend to the word 'nigger', however, which each of these three collectors includes in his version. Modern shanty culture is on the whole benign and liberal; but the fact remains that two of the most charged words in the English language were fully incorporated within the shanty lexicon: 'cunt' and 'nigger'. Whereas the first was eradicated as soon as the practice of collecting commenced, it's both instructive and chastening to observe that the second persisted (even among sensitive, sympathetic men such as Hugill) far longer than one would believe possible. Academic discourse, concerned with accuracy and authenticity, hauls in one direction; contemporary performance, concerned with morality and decency, heaves in another.

8 Cecil Sharp and Stan Hugill prefer 'Bowker', but I've stuck with the spelling given by Lloyd, Doerflinger, Captain Whall, Richard Terry, John Sampson, and Stuart Frank. The last named here, incidentally, identifies the 'rock and roll' mentioned in the first line of 'Johnny Boker' as the ancestral derivation of the term rock 'n' roll!

9 Gallus Meg was a notoriously dangerous character, noted for her ferocity when ejecting obstreperous sailors from Manhattan's Hole in the Wall bar. According to Herbert Asbury's *Gangs of New York* (1927), Meg kept a jar containing the pickled ears she had bitten off these unfortunates.

10 Harker went on to dedicate an entire book to the demolition of what he termed 'fakesong' – the proposition (as described by Steve Roud) that folk song never existed 'as a definable category of vernacular culture, but was a construct of the middle classes created for their own purposes, and commercial gain'.

11 Most commentators, incidentally, opt for an e-less spelling, although Hugill gives the Irish/American 'whiskey' in his *Shanties and Sailors' Songs*, as does David Proctor; Sampson dodges the issue by spelling it with a 'e' in his contents list, and without in the actual text. Folk supergroup Bellowhead covered this song as 'Whiskey is the Life of Man' on their album *Matachin* (2008).

12 There is, of course, also the accent – shared equally between Robert Newton's West Country rendition of Long John Silver in Disney's 1950 version of *Treasure Island* and Johnny Depp's Keith Richards-inspired Jack Sparrow from the *Pirates of the Caribbean* franchise.

13 Visitors to the south end of Paradise Street today, near the Liverpool One shopping centre, may notice large green, wrought-iron gates serving as a street sculpture. They belonged originally to the Liverpool Sailors' Home, opened in 1852 and built in the ornate style of a neo-Tudor palace (see vignette illustration, page 145). The landmark building remained in service until 1969, having provided lodgings over the years to thousands of sailors from across the world. It was demolished in the 1970s.

# PICTURE CREDITS

The cover artwork and the illustrations on the following pages were created by Jonny Hannah especially for *Sailor Song*: 1, 3, 4, 5, 21, 29, 39, 45, 55, 79, 85, 99, 115, 117, 120-121, 129, 139, 147,

© Jonny Hannah 2020

All other illustrations are from the collections of the British Library except the following:

**Page 8** National Library of Ireland; **13, 119** De Maus Collection, Alexander Turnbull Library, National Library of New Zealand; **27** Bancroft Library, University of California Berkley; **33, 152** New York Public Library; **36, 59, 89** Brodie Collection, La Trobe Picture Collection, State Library of Victoria; **37, 106, 107, 125** Library of Congress, Prints and Photographs Division, Washington, DC; **43, 47, 51, 72, 81, 124** Rijksmuseum, Amsterdam; **93** Collection of Rear Admiral Ammen C. Farenholt, USN(MC), 1931. U.S. Naval History and Heritage Command Photograph; **128** National Maritime Museum, Greenwich.

# ILLUSTRATION INFORMATION

**Page 6:** Sovereign of the Sea, engraving by Jacques La Grange, from Helen La Grange, *Clipper Ships of Great America and Great Britain, 1833–1869*, 1936; **8** North Quay, Drogheda, c.1860–1883; **9** *The Great Western of the U.S. Black Ball Line*, by Antonio Jacobsen, 1916; **10** details from Henri Paasch, *From Keel to Truck... Dictionary of Naval Terms*, 1908; **12** sailors working on deck, ship and date unknown; **13** on board the ship *Garthsnaid*, 1920, sailors securing a section of the foresail which had come free in heavy weather; **14** a 'Jolly Sailor' Victorian Valentine card, 1845–50; **15** a Victorian Valentine card, 1845–50; **17** *Watching the Height of the Waves*, from *The Graphic*, 18 March, 1871; **18** Illustration from the front cover of 'The Keel Row Schottische', composed by J.G. Jones, 1873; **23** *Poor Jack*, illustration by George Cruikshank from Charles Dibden, *Songs, Naval and National* (1841); **25** *Taking in Sail*, engraving by Jacques La Grange, from Helen La Grange, 1936; **27** sailing card for the clipper ship *California*, depicting scenes from the California Gold Rush, c.1850; **31** *A Hundred Tons of Despair are Churning the Oceans*, illustration by A. Webb from 'The Glamour of the Arctic' by Arthur Conan Doyle, published in *The Idler*, July 1892; **33** 'Mary Jane', sheet music, 1901; **35** Red Jacket, by Jacques La Grange, from Helen La Grange, 1936; **36** 'The *Imperator Alexander* bends to it', a deck view of a rolling ship, between 1885 and 1920; **37** *A Clipper Ship in a Hurricane*, lithograph by Currier & Ives, between 1856 and 1907; **41** *British Grog*, from a sketchbook entitled *Flights of Fancy* by John Frederick Herring Junior, 1831; **43** detail from a print relating to the first night of the Amsterdam Fair, 1857; **47** *Sailor in the Rigging*, watercolour by Herman Heijenbrock, 1904; **48** Chrysolite, by Jacques La Grange, from Helen La Grange, 1936; **51** detail from a print relating to the first night of the Amsterdam Fair, 1857; **53** *The Lads of the Ocean*, print by Isaac & George Cruikshank, 1805; **57** *A Famed Smuggler, Will Watch, Kissed His Sue*, illustration by V. Whall from W.B. Whall, *Ships, Sea Songs and Shanties*, 1910; **59** unbending a foretopsail and sending it down, on the *Loch Etive*, between 1885 and 1914; **60–61** details from Henri Paasch, 1908; **62** *Pits and Pitmen – Coal Whipping in the Pool*, illustration from *The Graphic*, 25 February, 1871; **64** 'The Sailor's Dream', composed by John Pridham, 1899; **66** details from Henri Paasch, 1908; **67** *The London Pool*, illustration by Gustave Doré from *London: A Pilgrimage*, 1872; **69** *Miss Kitty & the Bag*, by George Cruikshank from Charles Dibden, 1841; **71** *Then the Can, Boys, Bring, We'll Drink and Sing*, by V. Whall from W.B. Whall, 1910; **72** details from *The Difficult Passage*, anonymous print, c.1894; **75** Surprise, engraving by Jacques La Grange, from Helen La Grange, 1936; **77** *Meg of Wapping*, by George Cruikshank from Charles Dibden, 1841; **81** *The largest war ship, called* den Eendracht, Dutch print, 1704–1757; **82** *I'm Bound Away to Leave You*, by V. Whall from W.B. Whall, 1910; **87** *A Narwhal*, illustration from 'Life on a Greenland Whaler' by Arthur Conan Doyle, published in *The Strand Magazine*, January 1897; **89** The four-masted barque *Olivebank* in the North Atlantic, on starboard tack, between 1882 and 1922; **91** *Saturday Night at Sea*, by George Cruikshank from Charles Dibden, 1841; **93** Captain Raphael Semmes, *Alabama's* commanding officer, standing by his ship's 110-pounder rifled gun during her visit to Cape Town in August 1863, with his executive officer, First Lieutenant John M. Kell, in the background, standing by the ship's wheel; **95** *There's a Whale-Fish' He Cried*, by V. Whall from W.B. Whall, 1910; **97** *With Her Pistols Loaded She Went Aboard*, by V. Whall from W.B. Whall, 1910; **101** *Shenandoah: The White Man Loved the Indian Maiden*, by V. Whall from W.B. Whall, 1910; **103** *Heaving the Lead*, illustration from J.A. Atkinson, *A Picturesque Representation of the Naval, Military and Miscellaneous Costumes of*

*Great Britain*, 1807; **105** *The Packet Ship*, illustration by Gordon Grant from Henry B. Culver, *The Book of Old Ships*, 1924; **106** *Clipper Three Brothers, 2,972 tons: The largest sailing ship in the world*, lithograph by Currier & Ives, 1875; **107** *The fully rigged ship Mary L. Cushing*, c.1880; **109** *Tightening the Tiller Ropes*, illustration from *The Graphic*, 18 March, 1871; **111** *18th-century sailors*, illustration from Charles Rathbone Low, *Her Majesty's Navy*, 1890–93; **113** *On Board an Emigrant Ship – The Breakfast Bell*, illustration from *The Graphic*, 13 September, 1834; **119** *'Rigging and sailors'*, c.1900, David de Maus; **123** *All Hands on Board, Our Boatswain Cries*, by V. Whall from W.B. Whall, 1910; **124** detail from *The Life of the Naval Sailor*, anonymous print, 1875–1903; **125** *Holy-Stoning the Deck*, illustration from James Otis, *The Cruise of the Enterprise: being a story of the struggle and defeat of the French privateering expedition against the United States in 1779*, 1902; **127** *Emigrants Arrival at Cork – A Scene at the Quay*, illustration from *The London Illustrated News*, 10 May, 1851; **128** *Anne Jane Thornton, The Female Sailor*, anonymous print; **131** song score 'The Pride of the Ocean', composed by Thomas E. Williams, 1852; **133** Dreadnought, engraving by Jacques La Grange, from Helen La Grange, 1936; **135** Flying Cloud, engraving by Jacques La Grange, from Helen La Grange, 1936; **136** *The boat was run through the surf to the beach*, illustration from Frank R. Stockton, *Buccaneers and Pirates of our Coasts*, 1898; **135** *The great merchantman was captured*, from Frank R. Stockton, 1898; **141** *The pirates climbed up the sides of the man-of-war as if they had been twenty-nine cats*, from Frank R. Stockton, 1898; **144–145** plan of Liverpool by J. Rapkin, 1845; **148** Liverpool Docks, from Élisée Reclus, *The Earth and its Inhabitants: Europe*, 1878–94 (*Volume IV: The British Isles*, 1881); **149** Lightning, engraving by Jacques La Grange, from Helen La Grange, 1936; **151** *Tars Carousing*, by George Cruikshank from Charles Dibden, 1841; **152** *Marine Artilleries. 1862*, anonymous illustration of a Spanish naval uniform, 1910; **153** *Heaving the Lead*, from Charles Rathbone Low, 1890–93.

# ACKNOWLEDGEMENTS

My thanks to all the people with whom I've sung the songs included in this book over the past 30 years and more: the five other members of the Rock Light Rollers – Bob Brand, Paul Corcoran, John Edwards, Phil McGinity and Mike Penny; the members of The Full Shanty (the LJMU shanty choir) – Ryan Byrne, Lushiqi He, Jane Hogarth, Janine Melvin, Joe Moran, Maryjane O'Leary, Seamus O'Leary, Andrew Sherlock, Lucinda Thompson and Jade Thomson. Thanks also to Tom Wilson and all the staff at the Liverpool Arts Bar; to News from Nowhere, Liverpool's Radical Book Shop, for supporting my music over the years; to Ian Prowse for inspiration; to Ian Lewis for helping with the transcriptions, and for 20 years of patient musical collaboration. Thanks to my four children for putting up with such an uncool dad; and to my wife Stacey for constant love and support.

The principal sources that I used in my song annotations are: William M. Doerflinger (1951), James N. Healy (1967), Stan Hugill (1961, 1969, 1977 and 2006), A.L. Lloyd (1967), Douglas Morgan (2013), David Proctor (1992), John Sampson (1927), Cecil Sharp (1914), Laura Smith (1888), Richard Terry (1921, 1926) and W.B. Whall (1910). Full bibliographic details of these sources, as well as some other useful materials, may be found in the Further Reading and Listening.